A Year at Polverras

A Year at Polverras

Sylvia Ouston

Tabb House

First published 1984

Tabb House, 11 Church Street, Padstow, Cornwall PL28 8BG

ISBN 0 907018 25 4

Printed and bound in Great Britain by
A. Wheaton & Co. Ltd, Exeter

CONTENTS

INTRODUCTION

WHEN, in 1982, I re-read the narrative that follows, unearthed from among other almost-forgotten papers, it made me feel old, even older than I really am. The last fifty years have brought drastic outward changes to the Cornwall it describes. At the same time, an underlying spiritual continuity – may it survive massive attacks of the present-day – still makes one feel a presence of the men who chiselled wayside granite crosses on behalf of our earliest saints.

It was in the early 1900s that my part-Cornish grandmother returned to Cornwall to settle in a small and ancient seaside town. Only the doctor and two or three local notabilities then possessed motor-cars; a man lit the street lamps by hand every evening; no respectable housewife dared leave a scrap of washing visible on her line on a Sunday. I remember my elders saying that the old Cornish language was long dead, but that Breton fishermen who landed for a Saturday pub-crawl or shopping spree found our dialect home-like enough for fluent haggling. Of course, the First World War speeded up the evolution of daily life, even in Cornwall.

We moved to Devon in 1914, just before my grandmother's death. In 1918, our aunts brought my sister and me back to Cornwall, to live in a succession of country cottages. We did notice some slight changes; and from then on into the early 1930s talk of coming 'Progress' was constantly increasing. However, most people took the Cornishness of Cornwall for granted, as a permanent quality: a few farsighted patriots, who warned that someday it would perish if not defended, were generally written off as cranks.

Indeed, Progress seemed in no great hurry.

For instance, so long as the thirty mph speed limit persisted the still moderate number of visiting motorists adapted themselves to our winding roads, and I can recall hardly any widening schemes. One could walk, relaxed, on a wet dark night, even down the middle of a 'turnpike', with no fear of having to leap for one's life into the puddles alongside.

We hired a horse-cab to meet visitors arriving by train. Some farmers' wives and daughters still drove spanking ponies in open jingles: box-like vehicles high-slung on two wheels. Anyone good at catching donkeys could go and borrow one from the motley herd that grazed young furze and tussocky grass on the common.

There were already architectural eyesores in some beauty spots, but no large-scale alien developers had yet run up housing estates. Stone was becoming expensive, so a few people were trying out wooden bungalows as post-war homes, while concrete blocks were a more popular novelty. If you could face life without any modern amenities, you might still hope to buy a stone-and-cob cottage for a few hundred pounds.

This last fact partly accounted for the curious influx of unattached 'up-country' women, mainly unmarried 'reduced gentle-women', part of the feminine surplus left by the war to end wars. They came singly or in pairs, and were an interesting assortment. A few of the over-fifties with tiny incomes filled in their days by doing nothing in particuar. But the majority were active. Some wrote, painted, or wove; some flung themselves into learning pottery, or 'went on the land'. The most impetuous of the smallholders were those without cautionary experience in the Land Army. They were keen to try anything: fowls, ducks, geese, goats, rabbits, bees, bulbs, early vegs. Dauntless, they rigged up outhouses, with many nails and some string; they would attempt singlehanded (though perhaps only once) to open a hive. It seldom mattered much if their smallholding made no profit, merely providing food to supplement bread-and-marge. They learned a new outlook. The keeping of livestock taught them that Nature expresses devotion, strife, fatality. The immigrant ladies' eyes began to radiate serenity, while weather-worn wrinkles crept over their cheeks; they were too tired to bother any more with face cream at night.

Some of these settlers gave up and went back across the Tamar, but a good few stayed and eventually died among us, beloved as good neighbours.

Their advice was sought, as it was unbiased by local family ties. And because they had 'schooling', in those times when there was no radio or TV to proffer belated education, they were thought to be cleverer and wiser than they often really were.

The narrator in my story, though more prosperous than many, and here only on a short-term basis, is a sample of the species.

To some modern readers she may appear a prim and patronising person. This is inevitable. As outlooks and the manner of expressing them change, so each generation in turn becomes a 'period piece' to those that follow. Someday, the now-prevailing attitudes towards, say, religious observance or one-parent families, may seem alien.

Bar geese, my family went in for all the allegedly money-making livestock listed just now. Our two aunts were spinsters. We had been pretty poor for years past, but otherwise could be classed with the post-war New Poor. Nevertheless, because Cornwall had already been home to us, we felt different from and blessed above the newcomers. Up to a point we belonged, they were foreigners.

One thing that often puzzled them but came naturally to us was the Cornish code of social values. In England, there was much talk about the breakdown of class distinctions. In Cornwall such change was hardly perceptible, simply because the distinctions always had been less rigid and based on less materialistic grounds. For my grandmother's neighbours there had been 'gentry' and 'real gentry'. The former were expected to have money and at least a modicum of manners. Real gentry might be down to their last pennies, but they could dress like scarecrows and shovel muck without losing pubic respect; that is, so long as they lived up to the general code of ethics, and were courteous towards all. One seldom heard such condescending terms as 'the masses' 'peasants' or 'my good man'. Real ladies found it normal to address the plumber, the postman and so on, as Mr. No doubt historians could calculate how much these attitudes owed to our past: we had had few great feudal overlords, and the chiefs of small communities are judged by what they are, not by what they possess. In any case, this blend of democracy and aristocratic values made a Cornish upbringing a good start for mixing easily, at varied levels, with people all over the world.

One remaining nicety of division, however, did greatly influence our lives. At the village school, we 'would learn to speak like the born village children'; and in those days there was no BBC to inculcate standard English in and out of lesson hours. Our aunts could not afford to send us into town and pay fees, so they placated the occasional inquiring Inspector by employing a local governess for a few hours every week; and my sister and I grew up still surreptitiously doing addition on our fingers and without a single exam to our credit, though with inquisitive minds.

But how good, how full was our free life! We walked field paths and cliffs, alone or together, at all hours from early morning to moonlight. In their seasons we picked wild primroses and black-berries and proudly sold them for a few pence per bunch or pound. Battered second-hand bicycles in due course extended our range; we would dump them anywhere, against a hedge, a shop, a rock, confident that on our return from some long scramble they would be there intact, down to the pump. Few bad characters came to Cornwall, then still difficult to get away from speedily. Now and then there were warnings of a tramp being around, and one might encounter him, a hairy, weary and meek old man, busy, he too, picking blackberries or beachcombing.

Our teens sped on. We began to hold long earnest debates about make-up, satins, and silk stockings for our glamorous future, but, as always since the War, we were dressed mainly from parcels of 'nearly new' sent by kind London friends. Brambles and furze quickly wrecked this attire, so we patched woolly stockings with pieces cut from older woolly stockings and went out in ripped-up coats to cut bracken as bedding for the goats. Even when dressed up for church, folk-dancing, or a tea-party, we must have looked rather uncouth in an era that did not know blue jeans.

In the mid-1920s egg prices slumped and the dealer was paying only two shillings apiece for young duck carcasses. I renounced my intention of becoming the West Country's leading poultry farmer. Moreover, beyond the winter dances in our local tin hall, the summer cycle-rides to the nearest theatre (the return, four miles, slowed by fear of meeting a policeman and being arrested for non-functioning front lights), beyond these thrills a wider life was calling. Through advertisements in *The Lady*, I went away to three successive posts; as goat-girl, poultry-girl, and - the most disastrous - resident lady home-help. None of these afforded Life as described by my favourite authors, Emile Zola, Robert Service, and Jack London. So I emigrated to Canada, on an assisted passage – £6.10s including the transcontinental train.

After less than two years I was back, with psychological indigestion. Probably this ailment was what led me to believe I had been born to Write.

A new friend took me to London, and guided my awkward steps into free-lance journalism. But the slump of the '30s was beginning. The shrunken newspapers had no space for outside contributions. My friend fell ill and decided to leave the city for a while. We were both flat broke. "Go home to Cornwall", my friend bade me, "and try to write, but on a subject you really know and love."

There could be only one answer.

Absence had given a kind of historical perspective to the life of my childhood, still present though many aspects of it were; had made me aware of much I had not realised before, such as the music in Cornish voices, the way the cottages stand rooted in the ground as though they had been there forever, the innate graciousness of cottagers among whom were still some who could barely read or write, the all-pervasive influence of church or chapel. And two generations of my family were there to help, to correct interpretations that my rawness and new outlook might lead astray.

NOW I can only apologise if any readers find duplicates of their own names. The characters are, of course, as utterly fictitious as is usual in this type of book. If, for me, behind the masks of imaginings, changed relationships and mixed-up traits, real people stir, then, whether they were dear friends or known only by hearsay, I thank them for their share in my youth. All are dead or lost track of.

Half-a-century has passed, and in our present Cornish cottage my sister insists: "You *must* start sorting out those old papers; they'll be such a nuisance to your heirs."

1

REFUGE

WELL! At last I could pause and take stock of the Cornish refuge that would be mine for many months. How many, precisely, depended on doctors' verdicts: with the private hope of soon being hale and hearty enough to enjoy it fully but not to leave it, I had rented the cottage for 'at least a year'. One does not care to number in advance the days of the fulfilment of a dream. Childhood holidays in Cornwall, all spent in guest-houses, had shown me little of the practical workings of daily life. This was going to be different, enlightening.

It had taken longer than reckoned-on to arrive, find stowage for my boxes and help the delivery-man from the neighbouring town to arrange a few objects bought as supplements for my partly furnished dwelling. Everything was here now, except the writing-desk from my London home, included as a self-indulgence. That unusually convenient little writing-desk would stand in my bed-room exhaling memories, almost like a sentimental companion, and with the advantage of never talking at wrong times.

It was travelling alone. Misadventures had befallen it; 'not while on *our* line', the local station staff – Great Western and proud to be – had stressed to me that morning, when arranging for its conveyance by the afternoon bus to the Churchtown, Polverras, about a mile from my cottage.

By now, it was late afternoon. I stifled longings for a cup of tea, opened the front door, and from the granite threshold-slab looked around. What bliss! Peace, Strength, Comfort; surely they were all here, ready to repair a rather battered personality.

Chy Byghan, the 'little house', was a four-square granite cottage, with two rooms up, two down, under a slate roof with a squat chimney at each end and small-paned windows bright with white paint. I stroked the outside wall. They felt eternal, these stones, sisters to the boulders lying out there on the moor with the quartz in them sparkling under the declining sun. Golds were enriching the greys, silvers, and neutral tints of the scene: gold sky above the headland that shielded the bay on the west side, gold of sparse moorland furze-blossoms and the lichens on my roof, golden gleams even from the broccoli-stumps piled up, with sea-weed, to make manure, in an adjacent large field.

Low on the slope, where the cliff almost overhung a sandy cove, were other enclosures, about the right size for a dolls' farm. Each had its stone walls, and was further sheltered by evergreen windbreaks of veronica or escallonia. From one the breeze brought me a whiff of early violets. In the next, anemone flowers, red, white, purple, shone out from neat rows of foliage. The third was dug but empty, perhaps awaiting early potatoes. Down in that direction, whisps of chimney-smoke marked out my nearest neighbours' cottage, some two hundred yards away. My landlord's farmhouse, Boskew, considerably further off and to the east, stood, big and bleak, among many acres of pasture; inland from it, the ruined engine-house of an abandoned tin-mine displayed its jagged edges against the sky.

My only previous visit here had been rushed, between trains, and under escort by a house-agent. I had clinched the deal impulsively, spurred by the agent's hints of rival enquirers, who sounded to me unfit for this haven for idealists. As yet, I had not even inspected my outbuildings.

The one that held my provision of coal proved to be a former pig-sty: upside-down pyramids of snails were hibernating in its upper angles. Next to it, a big clean shed housed a mangle, a wooden scrubbing-board, a small tin bath, and a copper the right size for a large family's laundry. I counted my paces to the back door; eight only, most convenient for fetching coal. However, there were thirty-one from the front door to the earth-closet sheltered by fuschias and which, with its door ajar, gave a charming view of hart's-tongue ferns. Mental note: gum boots; keep them under mackintosh and sou'wester to be hung in my passage.

By now there was chill in the air. My craving for tea grew more acute. Indoors again, I had just picked up the kettle when somebody knocked.

My caller was a girl of about twenty, thoroughly countrified-looking, yet with something distinctive in her poise and her puritanically-plain style of dress.

She began shyly:

"Do please excuse me, Miss – ?"

"Barton."

"For disturbing you, Miss Barton. I am Ann Praed. And I haven't been able to find out anywhere whether a donkey-cart has been here by now."

"All I'm waiting for is a writing-desk."

"Ah! that's it! They did say, to Churchtown, they could feel a flat top and drawer-handles through the packing. It was all gone from sight by the time I got there. Bus had been late, and the butcher's, where parcels for this-way may be left, was closing early, for him to go on a family visit. So he hastened to get everything sent on. Oh dear!"

"Why?"

"There's a package from the vet, for Mrs Reynolds of Boskew; *that* couldn't wait. And your being so near, and perhaps worrying, they naturally loaded up yours too."

"Don't *you* worry – "

"But, Miss – Barton, excuse me: you see, it's our donkey, and Father driving. My poor father is sometimes very – wandering. When he leaves the donkey take charge, they just come straight home, but other times – So I can't calculate. But they should be along any moment now."

"Come in and wait," I invited.

Our chat lagged at first; my visitor was a little constrained, and clearly anxious. Then I happened to ask if there was a fieldpath to the Churchtown.

"Oh yes. It has church stiles too, so you will find it easy. They're always flat, for the coffins to pass over, in the old walking funerals. You will be wanting to know the service times, Miss, and I'm afraid I can't tell them exact. – Excuse me, but you would be Church – ?"

"Well," I replied, "I was brought up Church of England." This might, I sensed, be delicate ground. Sincerity was safest. I added: "By now, personally, I believe that faith itself is much more important than the frontiers men have set to the expressions of it."

The girl's face lit up, and now I noticed its one remarkable feature, the eyes: those glowing, intense blue eyes, recalling portraits of mystics.

She commented gravely: "What you say gives food for deep reflection, Miss. It do seem that more and more people are coming to think that way. These days, my mother's father wouldn't have had to creep in, by early dark, through the back door of the doctor's house – "

"Good gracious! Why?"

"You see, the doctor and his wife were lovely people who both knew Latin, and my grandfather, who was Minister to the Methodist church in the same place, just beyond Belruth, used to love to go and talk theology with them. But he daren't risk that one of his congregation should see him going in or out."

"Perhaps it was much the same on both sides."

"Miss Barton, aren't all we proud sinners scared awful easy! Why, the doctor's wife never set foot into my great-aunt's drapery shop because, with her husband a churchwarden, there might have been uncharitable talk."

"So it was quits!" I exclaimed, and wondered if this sounded flippant. "Change does come, with the generations," I added more sententiously.

"It's people as individuals that are harder, I'm learning that. You can't change a person except through a special grace." Ann's eyes suddenly lost their luminosity. She was listening to sounds of a commotion. "Above all, one's nearest and dearest," she ended abruptly, as though in spite of herself.

From outside came rumblings, rattlings, and roars of "Whoa, me dear, can't yer! Stand still, yer bloody cow!"

My visitor ran out into the dusk, and I followed. On the path beyond the garden gate, and each apparently trying to detach itself from the others, was a donkey, a two-wheeled cart, a small

black-moustached man who was vaguely waving his arms, and my
writing-desk, shrouded in hessian.

Ann was expostulating: "Father, how *could* you choose such a
roundabout way!"

"Yer fault, my girl, it is! If ee hadn't made me promise faithful to
be back for early supper and stay home, run up to Two Tinners
this evening, I could. But not break my word I wouldn't, not to a
dartar I'm that proud of, what stands up in pulpits preaching
golden glory. So I thought: I'll go round by The Chough."

"It's a mile further. And anyhow, they don't open till seven,
either."

"To Two Tinners they women be usually out gadding till
around six. But to Chough, back-kitchen door stands open and a
friend can go in for – for a bit of chat –"

"But Father dear, here was I, coming and disturbing this lady,
and she so busy and tired; and I had hoped, too, not to be late at
the Guild meeting tonight. Never mind, we will now lay our hands
to the plough."

Between us, we took down the writing-desk and carried it
indoors. Then father and daughter set off, she urging him on with
details of the star-gazey pie she had made for supper; he urging on
the donkey with peculiar terms of endearment.

I prepared candles for my bedroom, the paraffin lamp for
downstairs lighting, and my spirit lamp for boiling the kettle. And
now, that pot of tea...

The rainwater tank – my sole source of supply – stood opposite
the back door and was fed by a pipe that crossed over from the
roof-guttering. It was too tall for me to ascertain whether it had a
cover. Reminding myself that boiled water is sterilised, I bent to the
tap at the base and filled my kettle.

Fifteen minutes later, so much courage was coursing through
me with the hot tea that I determined to lug my writing-desk
upstairs, then and there. I had already measured it, and the top and
bottom of the stairs.

If praise is due to the ancient Greeks for their avoidance of
dead-straight lines, then how much more do we owe to the men
who built our old cottages! Part-way up, the space between the two

walls turned out to be exactly half-an-inch less than my desk could
pass through. The efforts and bumpings that finally convinced me
of this fact left me overwrought, a state in which defeat is apt to
engender rash zeal for taking up a new challenge.

A hot bath was now top-of-the-list in my yearnings. There was
no bathroom here, of course, but I pictured subtler voluptuous-
ness; that tin bath, brought in from the shed, full of lovely soft
rainwater and steaming in front of the fire, behind well-drawn
curtains. The kitchen-range looked a beauty. Its shining black
surfaces reflected numerous brass knobs. Coal, wood, and paper
had thoughtfully been left ready alongside it.

I had recently spent a fortnight helping an elderly cousin to
pack, for removal to a flat, from one of those tall old London
houses in which even 'dailies' no longer consented to slave. She
had put me in charge of the kitchen range and – to my surprise – it
had lit and burned readily every day. A proverb states: It takes a
fool or a philosopher to get a fire going. I now thought of myself as
a bit of a philosopher.

An extra door to the right of the new challenge suggested some
sort of *bain-marie*. I opened it, thrust my hand in and squealed
"Owwh!" The little cupboard was full of dry furze.

Undaunted, I tackled the main stove. First blithely, then
cautiously, I turned knobs, opened flues, shut them again. Flames
shot out at me, followed by black smoke. I twisted all the knobs in
new directions and the fire died. I repeated the performance with
some variations, and the fire blazed fiercely while the whole room
filled with smuts. – Quick, to the windows! – But they were firmly
sealed with stone-hard paint; former tenants had evidently breathed
enough fresh air during long days in the fields or at sea, and had
wished to exclude it from their home. Meanwhile, smoke was
drifting upstairs.

Again I flung the front door wide and went out onto the granite
threshold. This time, my eyes were smarting and my head was
swimming. This time, the outdoors was dark and cold. The breeze
had changed: instead of violets, it wafted me the reek of broccoli-
stumps and seaweed rotting together; a healthy smell, but one that

takes a little getting used to. Fog must have been setting in, for from out to sea came the wail of a warning horn.

And now, along the track below my garden and gradually growing louder, human voices were raised in strong appeal:

"Abide with me, fast falls the eventide,
The darkness deepens..."

In Cornwall, this noble hymn is not bound up with fear and melancholy, but resounds at the close of many a happy gathering; I did not realise this, however, and at that moment it struck me as unbearably poignant. I retreated indoors.

The smoke was worse than ever. Perhaps the chimney was on fire by now and I ought to find out how to call the Fire Brigade.

Coughing, I returned to the doorstep and, as the singing had ceased but footsteps could be heard, I called out: "Please, please – "

The trio who came hurrying up the garden path, lighting their way with two storm lanterns, were a smiling middle-aged woman and a lank, sandy man with a girl of about three perched on his shoulder. All were wearing near-Sunday-best clothes.

Even before they had introduced themselves as the Treloweths, my nearest neighbours, the woman whisked off her gloves and darted through the smoke.

"My dear life! Some muck you're in with that old slab!"

Her deft hands readjusted the brass knobs and as an organ changes its tune when the stops feel a master-touch, so did the erring stove respond. The coals began to glow and the smoke to dwindle.

"There! Don't ee vex yourself, my dear. You, Miss, aren't the first one from up-country to find a slab teasy to master. It'll need a few minutes to be sure this one is drawing proper – "

I dusted chairs and my befrienders sat down.

" – Should do. Swept the chimney was, the same day as ey cleaned out the water-tank. Some lucky for ee, all that dirty weather we've been having, for that tank must be good and full. – Wonder if they thought to put in a new toad?"

"A – ?"

"A toad. Keeps the water sweet, at least tis said to. To be on the safe side, John Peter here can look out for one for ee tomorrow, in the ditches."

"Thanks," I said, "but I – I" – how avert a reptilian tragedy? – "I daresay one will turn up for me in the garden."

"Anyhow, if ee leave the slab go cold now, I'll look in tomorrow morning and learn ee that. After what Ann Praed said to me when we was side by side at Guild meeting, I believe you won't think me making too bold. She said: 'This one's not one of they furriners whose neighbours never are good enough, so keeps themselves to themselves – till they goes away sudden, leaving pounds and pounds owing at the shops! Nor one of they that winds us up and winds us up to talk, and then makes a mock of what we tell! – Weren't they Ann's words, John Peter?"

"Er... um, n-not quite. Very c-careful choosing er words, A-Ann is," responded the man, speaking for the first time. A look of strain crept over his face and lent it a stupidity belied by intelligent eyes.

"Don't matter, that's what her must ave meant, though. – Acts a bit simple-like afore strangers, my husband do, Miss, ever since we had – a shock. – Cheer up, John Peter. That we came along of here just when this lady was a-choking and hollering was because ee would have us leave Guild meeting early, so as not to make Winnie Lizzie Treloweth here late to her bed."

"A son's child, Mr. Treloweth?" I enquired, meaning to put him more at ease.

A pause. His wife answered: "Us hasn't nothing but a daughter. Up to Plymouth she is, working."

Another pause. To end it, I narrated my troubles with the writing-desk.

It was John Peter's turn to display expertise. A quick, measuring glance at the staircase and the stranded piece of furniture, and he found the solution: unscrew the projecting top of the latter. "Do it r-right away, I could, with a s-crew-driver."

I had no longer the slightest recollection of where I had packed my tools. "Tomorrow – "

"Tonight," intervened Mrs Treloweth. "*I* understands, Miss, as when a woman is set on something, she's set: and you've told us as how ee was looking forward to seeing that there desk first thing on waking tomorrow. – Just run along home, John Peter, and fetch your tool-bag."

John Peter was absent for an unexpectedly brief time. When I answered his knock, not one man but three confronted me. The newcomers were a broad-shouldered greybeard and a lean, swarthy young man, a true black Celt, both of them in fisherman's garb.

"Do come in." (I had been saying that a lot this evening!)

The pair took off their sea-boots and entered respectfully on wool-stockinged feet.

Mrs Treloweth looked up from soothing the tired child on her lap.

"Ah, tis Uncle Joe Pender, and Harry Jago along of en. – Thought ee'd likely be back in cove soon, with tide what it is and fog coming up."

"Us fell in with John Peter almost just outside," said the older man, "and as I'd got a screwdriver in my pocket. – Tell ee truth, as I always have told truth these last three years since I got converted" – he gave a slight wink – "we was coming up around here to make sure all was as should be. For we saw lights and didn't know for sure when a new person was due in, us having been at sea four days."

"In Brittany waters," supplemented the youth.

"After pollock – and so on," precised the other quickly.

They all three turned their attention to the task, and with the dexterity that always makes me feel how useless I am compared to any handyman, they uncrowned the desk, coaxed it up the stairs, and installed it in the right place, with its top on again.

When they padded back, Joe Pender observed: "It's a nice place you have here, Miss. Dry."

"Oh, I'm relieved. But did you notice that big damp patch on the bedroom side wall?"

"That there's just a weeping stone, put in by mistake when they was building. Always sweat in damp weather, they do. Don't do no harm."

"If it were moved – "

"Part of that room would fall down for certain."

Mrs Treloweth exclaimed: "You saying that, Uncle Joe, reminds me that coming along I was thinking how this here cottage do look, from outside, a twin to the one what had its picture in all last week's papers. Some lucky as someone had that old photo laid by, for it all looks mazing different there now cottage is down mine."

"Subsidence," interpreted Joe Pender to me.

"A house can go down awful s-sudden when mine-gallery underneath g-gives way," enlarged John Peter. "Down into a y-yawning pit. Tis almost l-like a Judgement."

Here were possibilities new to me. I anxiously asked whether any workings of the nearby tin-mine were known to run under where we stood. Joe Pender reassured me: the nearest gallery ended in the adit that poured its reddish stream on to the beach, eastward, half-way along the cove.

Harry Jago volunteeered: "And the cave leading out of the adit is eastward again."

"What! Been nosing around that old cave, have ee, Harry?" demanded Mrs Treloweth, "after all the warnings Uncle Joe has given, that it's become a peril to life and limb. Finish the breaking of your poor old mother's heart, ee would, Harry, if ee got eeself killed that way. Wouldn't even sound too good, seeing twas known to be a smugglers' cave."

Joe Pender calmed her. "Now look ee, Mary-Liza, they old smugglers be all long dead and gone to story-books; and if there is nooks where us sometimes stows our – our gear, they're safe ones, as Harry knows."

His tone discouraged further discussion.

Winnie Lizzie was now wailing that she wanted to go home, and it seemed high time to start thanking my assembled helpers. Confused and tired, I opened wordily: "What a run of lucky chances today has brought me! I'm even indebted to my landlord, for I understand my desk got here today because an important parcel from the vet had to be delivered at Boskew."

"The vet?" echoed Mrs Treloweth, inquisitive. "I'll ask Glorermay. Shouldn't wonder if it weren't more of that there 'virility' stuff for the young bull what Mrs Reynolds is sending up-country. Mister couldn't fetch it himself, seeing he'd be away all today, with his car, to that conference on Local Ministration, or Administration, or such-like."

"Pow-wow about palm-oil, eh?" suggested Harry, and laughed.

Mrs Treloweth turned away from him and addressed me: "A leading figure in our public life, is Mr Reynolds, Miss."

Murmur behind her: "You poor suckers!"

She stiffened, swung round. "Harry Jago, ee'd best have left behind in Canada they unchristian foreign manners. Or else have stayed there with em. I won't stand for no grunting and glowering and making mock about Mr and Mrs Reynolds, after all their kindness and help to us at the time of – Winnie's trouble, and since. Have ee anything else to say, and is it fittier to hear?"

"I will say 'Sorry!', and 'Sorry!' to this lady too. Thinking out loud I was, that's all."

"Think the rest out loud, then, and have done with en."

The now exasperated young man reflected for a moment, then said slowly: "O.K. – I'd been wondering what price the vet would charge to poison a worn-out bull and a lame bitch."

The Treloweths exchanged puzzled looks.

Joe Pender took his nephew's arm. "Comst on, boy. When ee learns to put a peace on what can't be altered, ee'll be come of age. – Us'll move off now, for we'll have to rise by dark to start disposing of they – pollock, and so on."

A CHORUS of "Good-night"'s, and they were gone, all five of them. I was alone for the first night in my refuge.

I wiped lingering smuts from the spirit-lamp and made another pot of tea. Whatever was in my water-tank; live toad, dead toad, no toad; that tea tasted good.

Next, I did something I had not done for years and was never to do again under that roof. I wept, hard.

Perhaps it was just tiredness. Or an upsurge of emotions that had been gathering, always repressed, ever since the First World War. Kindness from strangers often breaks down barriers that have long stood fast, and everyone here was being kind to me.

All seemed in harmony here, too. No, not quite all. But in

every village one may expect at least one old toper. As for that strange, sarcastic youth, spiritual wounds received in the harsher New World might well not yet be healed.

So I hugged my glowing first impressions and pushed aside a suspicion that in seeking refuge from one set of human foibles and dramas I had pitched myself into another – *Kismet!* Tomorrow almost always modifies impressions. Which is another good reason for cherishing the best while they last; even if only while one climbs crooked stairs – to ten hours' sleep.

2

GLORERMAY'S ROMANCE

"YOU'LL be frightened to see the difference when they're scrubbed and whitewashed proper," predicted Mrs Treloweth, pointing to my kitchen rafters.

Apart from my recent disaster with the smoking stove, I had taken for granted that the cottage interior owed its mellow tints solely to age, not grime. Mrs Treloweth had undertaken to open my eyes. And since her exposure of five layers of decaying wallpaper under the yellow-and-blue one in the parlour, I respected her judgement.

"Trouble is," she went on, "I can't do they rafters for ee. Reaching up makes my head turn. And you can't trust no man or boy not to limewash over half the muck."

"What about the village girls?"

"There's some as would, but would just cadge on the paint and limewash. And tothers too proud to work for wages. Clara Curno from The Two Tinners, now, she did her mother's ceilings proper. But she's that set on being a lady and not soiling her hands that she had to be fair driv to it. Glorermayallen would have made a good job of en."

"What name?"

"Glorermayallen, Mrs Jim Allen's eldest. Christened after they film stars she was, and we call her Glorermay for short. But she works to Boskew farm every day, and I doubt she'd have the time to come on here."

"Here is our friend," I interrupted, seeing through the open door Joe Pender's burly figure coming up the garden path.

He entered, and handed me a clammy parcel wrapped in newspaper. "A little present of pollock for ee, Miss Barton," he explained.

"Hullo, Uncle Joe! Do ee know what time Glorermay leaves Boskew evenings?"

"Six or thereabouts."

"That's some lucky. She'll be able to give ee an hour every evening, Miss Barton, my dear. Proper little worker she is. Only girl that Mrs Reynolds will have for maid since our Winnie went away."

"Or only one as will work for Mrs Reynolds," grunted Joe Pender.

"Well, there is some as do call Mrs Reynolds a proper old slave driver without a soft spot in her heart, 'cept for her pedigree cattle. A fair cross for Mr Reynolds, and him so pious and yet so chummy-like. But I wouldn't say nothing against him nor her either after the way they've helped my Winnie. – Well, Miss Barton, you'd best catch Glorermay when she comes by here with Mrs Reynolds' cows tomorrow morning."

AND SO, next morning, I watched by the field gate.

A soft trampling and a softer rustle of deep breaths heralded the cows on their way to pasture. Down the road, round the bend of the hedge they came, sixteen golden-coated Guernseys with the slender, finely-drawn limbs of thoroughbreds, and dark eyes mild as those of fallow deer. From side to side of the road they sauntered, stopping to crop here a primrose plant, there a spray of still green honeysuckle; unhurried, aware that, in these parts, road priority was theirs. A few yards behind the herd came a single cow, even sleeker than the others. Besides her, one arm thrown over her neck, walked a girl of about sixteen.

Glorermay was short, thickset, muddy-complexioned. She walked with a hit-and-miss gait, throwing out sometimes the right leg, sometimes the left, in a wide curve, then jerking the other forward to catch up. Short, lank locks of black hair dangled over her forehead. But she looked cheerful, intelligent, and clean.

Refusing ninepence an hour as more than her work was worth, she agreed to clean and whitewash all my rafters for five shillings the lot.

As she was about to move on, I remarked: "What a pretty cow."

"My pride and joy, aren't you, Betsy? – She was sickly as a calf, for all she has a pedigree, Miss. I helped to raise her. And now that she's going to have a calf of her own, Mrs Reynolds lets me look after her special-like, if I work half-an-hour extry in the house to make up. When she's poorly, she half kicks her stall down rather than take her drenches from any but me. Don't ee, my handsome?"

The cow turned her head, rubbed her muzzle against the girl's knee, and expresssed impatience by a stamp of a front foot and a swish of her tail.

"Just like a dog, isn't she, Miss? She's fretting to be getting along now, so excuse us."

Hurrying to keep up with her friend's stride, Glorermay vanished down the lane.

A WEEK LATER, all my rafters being spotlessly clean, I engaged Glorermay to do daily jobs about the garden and house.

As a maid she proved efficient, though by no means ornamental. She was heavy-footed but not heavy-handed. Though always untidy-looking herself, she never left a trace of untidiness behind her; and her passion for cleanliness satisfied even Mrs Treloweth.

Every evening at 6.10 she reached me, panting after her run from Boskew Farm. Every evening at 7.10 she hurried away home to a tumble-down cottage on the moor above the village, there to begin another half-day's work, scrubbing and washing, and mending for eight younger brothers and sisters; tasks left to her by a mother much of whose time was spent reading novelettes or going to the 'pictures' at Belruth. She always came and went from work alone. On the Sunday chapel parades in which other girls appeared in groups or with their sweethearts, she walked by herself, or else pushed a perambulator laden with small children. She never mentioned any friend save the cow Betsy. But so cheerful, so contented did she seem, that she had worked for me for three weeks before I discovered her yearnings for romance.

It was a Thursday, Polverras' early-closing day.

Glorermay, looking out of the kitchen back window, exclaimed: "Oouuh! Look there, Miss."

I looked.

"That's Billy Berriman and Clara Curno going down Cove on his new motor bike. Seems like she may mean to go with him steady till she's found a fellow with a real car. Don't Billy Berriman look some smart since he started working to shop, Miss? The way he sticks his hair down with that there scented stuff."

"I wish he thought more of his work and less of his appearance," I retorted. "While I gave him my last order, he kept his eyes glued to some new ties a traveller had brought; and he's sent me soda for flour, and allspice for rice."

"Spect it's his fine ways that have caught Clara's fancy. Shouldn't be frightened if he had taken her to Belruth today, to get a new dress for the dance next Thursday."

"Are you going to that dance?"

"Haven't got no boy to take me."

"Then let's look around for the right one. Would Harry Jago do?"

Glorermay shook her head. "I ain't proud, but I wouldn't be seen around with a fellow of his reputation."

Ever since I had settled in, I had wondered why Harry Jago was held in ill repute. But a glance through the front window started my thoughts on another track. "Look, Billy Richards whom you work with at Boskew, is coming here. Would he suit you?"

"Lovely, Miss. But there ain't no hopes for me there."

"We will see."

I went to the door, to meet a stolid lad with a face the colour of, and with about as much expression as, an underbaked pasty.

"Brought a message for Glorermay," he announced.

"Billy, Glorermay must go to the dance with a really nice partner. Will you take her?"

"Huh. No. Haven't got no time for fooling." Billy Richards, as usual, spoke slowly and heavily.

"But Glorermay works as hard as you, yet she is ready for a little fun."

"Huh. Shows she ain't no better'n the other girls, after all. A feller what has set his heart on working and saving for a farm of his own had best keep off women."

"A farmer needs a wife's help."

"What a feller can look for and not find hereabouts is a girl fit to be a farmer's wife. - Tell Glorermay, will ee, Miss: Mrs Reynolds says she's to come an hour early tomorrow, to pluck chicken; and if she don't, she'll lose her day's wages. Them was Mrs Reynolds' very words."

And with that, Billy Richards turned on his heel.

Glorermay was in the passage, brazenly eavesdropping. "You see, the boys haven't no use for me, Miss. And I reckon I'm kept busy enough without them. Not but what I could do with one if they felt different."

She heaved a sigh, then resumed: "Never mind, Miss. I'll have my fun at Polverras Chapel Feast next Saturday. As it's to be in the field just between here and Mrs Treloweth's, I'll be able to slip off easy for my work here."

"Take a holiday. I'll pay you just the same."

"Oh-h Miss, that will give me another hour of it! And it's going to be some fine Feast: two roundabouts, five stalls of ice cream and ginger fairings, and six banners in the procession. And Belruth Brass Band, what you can hear from twice as far off as any other, is going to play - "

She was interrupted by Mrs Treloweth's arrival. "If ee don't mind, Miss Barton, I'll take that silver tea-pot you are lending me, so I can polish en up proper for the Feast. Saving me from shame, you are. I'd been fair dreading helping to pour out tea with my old cloam tea-pot, and all the neighbours seeing as how the spout's broke. - And Ann Praed has just told me of your giving five shillings for the Feast fund. Well, you wait till Saturday, and you'll find out how much store is set on your kindness."

ON FEAST SATURDAY afternoon, I was reading in the parlour when a tempest of instrumental sound suddenly filled the room. My first shock over, I recognised the 'Hallelujah Chorus'.

I went to the door. Outside, fifteen brass bandsmen were blowing and thumping, and behind, in a straggling crocodile, was the Procession. In its forefront stood Ann Praed, Mrs Treloweth, and John Peter, holding between them a large Temperance banner;

then the ranks tapered away through rows of youths and girls in their
Sunday-best to a tail of white-muslin-frocked or velvet-suited Sunday
School pupils. At least a hundred eyes were fixed on my cottage.

Over the garden gate swayed the Temperance banner.

"Some surprise for ee, eh, Miss Barton?" demanded Mrs
Treloweth in a stage whisper.

John Peter nudged her and cocked his head at me.

Ann Praed explained: "I asked them to play here first, before
going on to Boskew. It seems only right that a stranger should
have the first greeting."

I murmured thanks, and, including everyone from band-master
to the smallest Sunday School child in my gratitude, nodded
emphatically to right and left. The last chords rang out, band and
procession wheeled round.

As they moved away, a squat figure in a large white hat broke
from the ranks and ran towards me. It was Glorermay. "You'll
come up to Feast, won't ee, Miss?" she begged. "For we all feel
you're one of us, like, now you've had a tune."

So three hours later I went up to the 'Feast Meadow', to which,
after its round of complimentary calls, the procession had returned.

Hanging about the entrance gate was a group of youths and the
less respected local characters, among them Harry Jago, morose
and lonely-looking as usual. Two squabbling urchins ran out past
me, with Glorermay in pursuit of them.

Tea being over, the bandsmen were just settling down to work
again. Around them was a semi-circle of benches. On the central
one sat Ann Praed, and the stout benign-looking farmer and
tight-lipped woman leaning on crutches, the owners of my cottage,
whom I had heard described as "the rich Reynoldses of Boskew";
on the next, public personages – the postmistress, schoolmistress
and shopkeepers – were sorting themselves out; while the horns of
the crescent were occupied by mothers with babies, and a swarm of
small children letting off squeakers, or munching saffron 'harvest
buns' as big as their heads. Between the benches and the
fair-booths, the older boys and girls strolled about self-consciously,
in groups and pairs.

I had just sat down on the edge of the outermost bench when a young voice raised peevishly behind me made me turn my head. Side by side were standing Billy Berriman, decked out in a grey suit and lavender tie, and the deep-bosomed seventeen-year-old daughter of The Two Tinners.

"Getting hard of hearing, are you, Billy Berriman? I asked for a Neapolitan, and you bring me one of them penny cornets."

"Aw. They Neapolitans aren't wholesome."

"Then why did you buy me three of them last Thursday, to Belruth? What tis, you don't want to pay sixpence for it." Clara tossed her auburn curls. "Think any girl is so tickled to have ee that you can take her around on the cheap, eh?"

"Aw, I say now, you know tisn't that, Clara. Though you do have expensive tastes. An I got to keep something back from my wages to pay for this ere tie, and haircut, and my new socks, and to take you to the dance, come Thursday."

"Who said I was going to the dance with you?"

"You yourself."

"Well, I've changed my mind. I wouldn't be seen dead to a dance with such a conceited skin-flint."

"Awl right. I don't care – I'd as lief go to the dance with the first girl who comes through that there gate as I would go with you."

"Would ee really? – Prove it!"

Through the meadow gate ran a squat figure in a white hat, still pursuing the two tearful urchins.

Billy Berriman strode towards Glorermay.

Just then, Mrs Treloweth drew me aside. "Oh, Miss Barton, we're in some sore difficulty. Mrs Simmons, what was to have played the piano for the dance, is took bad with her back again and says she'll never be able to last out the whole evening. Would ee play tune and tune about with her, my dear? I've listened to ee a-banging of your own piano just like a real musicker."

My protests about being out of practice availed not. In the end, I consented.

THE FIRST THING Glorermay told me of on the Monday evening, even before reporting on the cow Betsy's health, was her invitation.

"Fancy Billy Berriman asking me!" she finished. "E told me as how he always had noticed I was different from the other girls he knows, but he hadn't liked to say nothing about it before. But I'm bothered about my dress – "

"What is wrong with it?"

"Oh it's a handsome dress; the yellow-and-white silk with the pink fringe what I paid two shillings for to the church Graveyard Fund Jumble sale last year. But there's an awful great ink-stain down the front. And Billy Berriman's that particular!"

I lent her an old blue silk tunic frock. The colour suited her, and what I lacked in breadth and she in height seemed to average out successfully. Dressed in this, Glorermay looked less ungainly than I had believed possible.

"It'll be some smart when it's trimmed," she pronounced, looking at herself in my long mirror.

"Those tucks are the trimming," I said hastily. "Wear it as it is now, and put just a little powder on your face."

"Tis a pity Mr and Mrs Reynolds are going to their cousin's to stay. And I promised the Missis faithful to stop late and lock up the dairy," sighed Glorermay, as she pulled off the dress with reverent hands.

By 8.30 the next evening, the dancing youth of Polverras was getting warmed up. The atmosphere of the first three fox-trots had been icy, only half-a-dozen couples finding enough confidence to take the floor and demonstrate their skill before neighbours. But a Paul Jones had broken the ice. It had filled the hall with a din of stamping feet, shaken down flakes of plaster from the walls, and set girls dancing together in order to encourage the more bashful youths who, under pretext of wanting to smoke, were huddled sheep-like near the door.

The Paul Jones had ended, and now the dancers, mopping their brows or powdering their noses, had retired to chairs ranged round the walls. I myself was resting from a turn at the piano and sitting next to Clara Curno, who had arrived just late enough to ensure a good 'entrance' for her new green satin dress.

A stir in the group near the door made me turn expectantly.

Glorermay entered.

She had tied a pink cotton sash tightly around her blue silk dress. About her neck dangled a string of artificial pearls, and another of glass beads. Over one ear was perched a small pink bow; over the other, a butterfly of false brilliants. Behind her came Billy Berriman, dressed correctly in black, his lips tightly set, his expression defiant.

As they passed us by, Clara Curno sniggered.

Billy Berriman turned on her. "I'll learn you manners," he told her in an undertone.

"Come on Mr Berriman. Music's starting again," urged Glorermay.

"Don't waltz, do ee, Miss Allen?"

"Oh ess. I can get round the room to anything if I hum to en. Dum, dum, dum, Dum, dum, dum."

A square-toed shoe trod on Billy Berriman's patent-leather one; a red hand reached up to his shoulder. Glorermay had taken the floor.

Most rustic young people at that time fought shy of the waltz, because it calls for more than a walking-step with, or without, variations. So the newcomers had plenty of room for their display.

When the last chord sounded, Billy Berriman wiped his crimson cheeks and suggested: "Aw I say. We'd best sit out the next."

"'Tis a shame to miss a fox-trot, Mr Berriman. And you just getting into my stride too."

Off they went again. Glorermay evidently believed that in a dance, guidance should be the woman's part. Like a frisky cart-horse yoked with a light hack, she dragged her partner with her, unconscious of the feet she trod on, the bodies she barged into, hip and shoulder foremost. As I looked at her face I thought of a tomato dipped in hot water; then seeing the joy in her eyes, I felt ashamed.

The first half of the supper dance was over, and the partners were sitting down to feast heartily on ices, sandwiches, and home-made cakes, when a stocky figure in corduroys entered the hall. It was Billy Richards.

He came straight up to me, his hobnails clanking on the polished floor. "Glorermay here, is she?"

I beckoned, and Glorermay came, bringing her partner in tow.

"Ullo, Billy Richards, come to join us after all, ave ee? We're having some grand time, aren't us, Mr Berriman?"

"Where's Boskew dairy key to?"

"I got en pinned safe in here." Glorermay tapped her breast. "What do ee want it for?"

"Betsy's drench. Keep it on the dairy shelf, don't ee?"

"What! Something wrong with my Betsy?"

"I found her took kind of paralysed when I went in to water the calves. John Peter thinks as she's going to drop her calf early."

"Telephoned vet, did you?"

"Yes. Ee was going off urgent to a pig somewhere. Said he can't get to Boskew afore late. Hurry up with that there key!"

Glorermay plunged her hand down into her bosom, drew out the key, and handed it to Billy Richards.

"All right. Leave ee to your jigging now."

"Billy – wait. Is – is Betsy real bad?"

"Worsen't I ever seen a cow."

"Stop a minute. I'm going to er with ee."

"Aw, I say what!" Billy Berriman grabbed her arm. "Leave a partner in the middle of the supper dance, let him look foolish eating his supper all alone – That ain't no way to behave!"

Glorermay hesitated, trouble and doubt stamped on her face.

"Coming?" asked Billy Richards.

"I'm some sorry, Mr Berriman," burst out Glorermay, "but Betsy don't like none but me around her when she's poorly. And tis my duty to see that all goes proper while Mr and Mrs Reynolds is away."

"This is the first time I've been seen around with you, Miss Allen; I'll make it the last if you chuck me for a darned old cow. Take your choice now; cow or me."

Glorermay stood shifting from foot to foot under the disapproving glare of both the youths: her lips trembled, tears filled her eyes.

With a shrug of his shoulders, Billy Richards strode away.

One look round at her partner, at the girls and boys listening and giggling on the chairs, then Glorermay ran hit-and-miss, hit-and-miss down the hall. She pulled her coat from its peg, and vanished at Billy Richard's heels into the street.

NEXT EVENING, I met Billy Richards sauntering up and down outside my garden gate.

"Glorermay be along any moment now, won't she?"

"Yes," I answered. "What happened to the cow?"

"Calved all right. But we had a night of it. Me and the vet and John Peter didn't leave her till three, and Glorermay, not until she started work."

It was half past six when Glorermay scuttled into the kitchen.

"I'm that sorry I'm late, Miss," she panted, "but Billy Richards wanted to speak to me particular out there. We're going to go together regular, him and me. And, oh Miss Barton, Betsy's had the andsomest little calf!"

"Congratulations!" I said. "Isn't your romance very sudden?"

"Tis all along of Betsy. Billy Richards said just now as how ee really made up his mind last night to ask me. He says – " Glorermay looked down coquettishly; "ee says as a girl what'll leave a dance for a cow will make him a suitable wife when ee's a farmer."

3

THE PREACHER

ANN PRAED had called in for some curtains she was to hem for me, and was waiting in the parlour while I fetched them.

On my return, I found her in front of my bookcase, dipping into Kant's *Critique of Pure Reason*, a gift from an erudite relative which, I confess, I had not read. My visitor turned round, blushing deeply.

"I beg your pardon, Miss Barton. Books are the one thing I'm inquisitive about. It's a hard job for me to get any serious ones here; philosophy and theology. And they do help me to think out my sermons."

"You preach! You who look only just out of school!"

"Indeed they all tell me I look terrible young. But I'm twenty-one years and three months old come Monday. And I've done a considerable bit of preaching at the chapels around here."

"What made you begin?"

"It just came. After Mother died, I kept on going to Chapel, though Father was teasy about it at first, as about my studying late at nights. Then, four years ago, one anniversary service away up beyond Belruth, the preacher had an epileptic fit right in the midst of his sermon. And the people got all bothered. Something had to be done. So I stood up and spoke to them," she explained simply.

"You were brave!"

"I didn't feel brave; I can even now remember how my knees were shaking under me. And they still do – until I get properly started. Next Sunday, when I'm to preach before the Circuit Superintendent who is visiting us, they will shake worse than usual, for it is to be right here in our own Chapel."

"Ah, – you don't like addressing your neighbours?"

"No. For I know that some of them are thinking: 'Look at Ann

Praed's conceit. Laying down right and wrong to us; she that can't even set her own father going straight'."

"You ought to get away from this district," I suggested.

The girl's eyes flashed, lighting up her whole face, and she answered eagerly: "Oh Miss Barton, that is my dearest wish. To go and train for mission work and to lead revivals; to speak to those who will listen with open minds! I've never been farther than Plymouth, but I wouldn't be afraid even of London. Polverras is like a prison to me. I – I just feel that so long as I am here, I shall never do justice to myself or my Call."

"Is the training a difficulty?"

"Yes. It would cost more than the fifty pounds my Aunt Jane in New Zealand left to me. Father's Navy pension and what he makes by dealing in vegetables and doing odd jobs all go for himself, and I can't save much from the little I earn by sewing."

"Have patience," I said. "Your chance is sure to come."

She answered wistfully: "I'm – doubtful. Sometimes I think it must be denied to me on purpose, as a sign it is only my vanity that sends my thoughts so far afield."

Looking down, she stood twisting her cotton gloves in her hands; strong, spatulate, forceful hands. Then the abrupt change I had witnessed once before came over her: she raised her head, her features hardened, the glow in her eyes was gone.

"Listen! That's Father. What can he be doing down here at this time of morning?"

We heard a raucous cry: "Brocoli! Taters! Leeks! Honions!"

Together we went out to the rough track where the now-familiar donkey-cart had halted. At the donkey's head stood William Praed, his face flushed and his gait unsteady.

Ann put a hand on his arm.

"Ullo, my little maid – Brocoli! Ta-ters! – Want some fine spring honions, M'am?"

"But look, Father, you have nothing but two cabbages left in the cart! Didn't you ever get to market and buy your new stock?"

"Aye. I got there right and proper. And met Jim Vellanoweth to The Golden Carn, just back from Newquay with his coursing dogs. But I minded my ead, I did. Said 'No' to the last pint Jim

offered me. Must have been afore that that I clean forgot the
market."

"Oh, Father! Well, we'll go back there later, together. Suppose
I take the money now."

The man rummaged in the pockets of his dirty jacket and drew
out five pennies and a half-penny.

"Blarsted if I can mind where that five shillin you gived me is
to." He pushed back his cap and scratched his head. "Oh, ess, I do
mind en. Me and Jim Vellanoweth had a game of darts, and I
didn't seem able to throw good today. But I'll make em back,
make em double and enough over to get ee a new hat, my girl.
Blarst me if I don't. – Git up, Bob;" he prodded the donkey; "yer
bloody grey'ound. – Taters! Bro-coli!"

Ann seized the donkey's forelock and, with her free hand,
steadied the man.

"Let go, little un. I got to go down village – "

"No, no, Father. Come along back home, and I'll change your
shirt and get you out a clean jacket."

As the trio turned back up the lane, I called out: "Think of that
chance which is sure to come, Miss Praed."

THE following Sunday evening, I set out for Chapel. Under my
arm were tucked Locke's *Human Understanding*, which, after
service, I meant to leave at Ann's cottage, and two identical hymn
books, neither of which, one being lent by Mrs Treloweth and the
other by Glorermay, had I dared to leave behind.

The field-path to the village was dotted with groups of people
walking sedately chapel-wards. The women creaked along in tight
shoes, with their new hats – all, no matter of what shape or size,
rammed on straight across the brows; the men looked hot and
constrained in their stiff collars and Sunday suits. The only person
who seemed his usual self was Harry Jago, who, in fisherman's kit,
hands in pockets, came swinging along from the opposite
direction.

He volunteered to turn back and carry my books. "Grand
evening for a walk, Miss Barton. But I guess you're going to sit
under a roof with a crowd of they other suckers."

"I am going to hear Miss Praed preach."

"So would Mother have done if she hadn't been lying in hospital again. She didn't ask me to go in place of her though. Understands, does Mother. – I guess ee won't get no harm listening to *that* preacher. Lives according to what she preaches, she does, which you can't say for all who stand up and spit out texts to Chapel."

"Perhaps you prefer church," I ventured.

"Me? Why, to church they puts the poor and sinful in the back seats to humble em, to chapel they puts em in front for the righteous to gape at. That's all the difference *I* see between their darned religions."

As usual, I was at a loss how to take this vehement youth, who shot forth his opinions and then seemed to wait hungrily for my replies.

He threw out his chest and looked about him at the flower-dotted hedges and the bay, opal-tinted in the evening light.

"By Golly, I'm not one of those as fancies there's God in Nature nor anywhere else. But I reckon they cliffs and fields is what keeps me sane in this gold-darned hole."

"You too do not like the village?" I was recalling Ann Praed's outburst.

"'Tis hard not to like the place when've been born and raised here. And when ee comes back to it after a great, bleak prairie farm in Canada where there're no hedges, nor trees, nor rocks with little ferns on em. But the folks here – "

He broke off. Rounding a corner, we had come in sight of Mrs Treloweth and of John Peter, who was holding in his arms what looked like a bundle of frilling.

"I'll bid ee 'Good evening', Miss," said Harry.

He thrust the books back into my hands and strode away. I was left wondering about these two, the young preacher and the young pagan, the only local people who showed discontent with their lot; wondering also at Harry's evident anxiety not to meet my neighbours.

John Peter's frilly burden was Winnie Lizzie who, in her starched muslins liberally threaded with ribbons, minute white cotton gloves, and straw bonnet loaded with daisies, looked like an overdressed doll.

"Three years old today, she is," Mrs Treloweth told me, "and being put to Chapel for the first time. We've kept her back this long for Ann Praed, so she can tell people later how the first sermon she ever heared was preached by an own cousin to her mother's aunt."

As we reached the main street, Joe Pender came briskly out of The Two Tinners. Then there was a noise of angry voices and, pushed forward by a strong pair of arms, William Praed staggered onto the road. The public house door closed behind him.

"They cursed Curnos!" the ejected man shouted, shaking his fist at the inn door and then following us. "Turning me out tonight! Tonight, when I be ready to spend the whole evening a-celebrating my Annie's preaching to her blessed Superintendent!"

"You'd prove your pride more proper by a-coming and hearing of her," said Mrs Treloweth severely.

"That's what I tell en," Joe Pender chimed in. "I don't mind admitting I'm not the chapel-goer I might be. But I wouldn't not show myself at my own sister's daughter's preaching; no, not for nothing."

"Get enough of Annie's tongue weekdays, I do," protested William Praed beerily. "Preaching bain't my line. But as tis Annie's, I'm proud of er for doing so andsome in it."

"Proud is something she can't be of ee," commented Mrs Treloweth.

"Annie knows er old Dad's all right, though ee don't go *er* way. And while she's laying down the law to Chapel, I'll be celebrating of er success to home. Got that ere what will last me till opening time," and he slapped a traitorously bulging pocket. "Come home along of me, won't ee, Joe?"

"No."

"Well, I got to hurry to wish the little maid good luck afore she goes," chuckled the old wastrel.

And he shambled off towards the lane that led to his cottage.

"Poor Annie!" remarked Mrs Treloweth. "To have her own

father seen around in that state, and when Superintendent's just
arriving, too!"

We had reached the white-washed chapel which, with its two
front windows surmounted by black painted arches, appeared to
gaze at the world with eyebrows forever raised in disapproval.

From a car drawn up in front of it there stepped a sleek,
dark-haired man, at whose approach the groups on the chapel
steps drew aside respectfully. Next came the tall, broad-shouldered
figure of Ezekiel Reynolds, who returned the smiles and nods that
greeted him on all sides. Last to leave the car was his wife. Stiff and
sombre, erect in spite of her crutches, she entered the building
without a glance to left or right. After them went we smaller fry,
some still chatting, but now in lowered tones.

Though it lacked ten minutes to service-time, the place was
already full. I recognized almost every face I knew in the village,
but there were many others I had never before seen; people from
outlying farms and hamlets to whom 'Chapel' was the one outing
in the week.

The green-washed walls were bare save for a coat-rack near the
entrance door. At the far end stood a platform with a chair and
reading-desk; on the step below this, a harmonium; and below
again, facing the aisle between the varnished benches, a kitchen
table covered with a spotlessly white cloth, and bearing a jam-jar
full of anemones. A sunbeam shining through the western window
touched the flowers and made them a beacon of loveliness,
gleaming out against their austere surroundings.

John Peter escorted me to the pew behind the one that the
Reynoldses and their guest occupied. Curious glances towards the
Superintendent, subdued whispers, and giggles among the children
ceased by degrees, and all eyes were fixed on a door behind the
platform.

"She's late," I heard Mrs Reynolds whisper acidly.

The Superintendent looked at his watch.

"It's seldom like this, Sir." Ezekiel Reynolds' undertone was as
genial as his wife's had been harsh. "Our preacher tonight has –
family troubles, Sir."

Once more, I took stock of the faces around me. Kindly,

willing-to-be-pleased, most of them. John Peter was leaning forward, hands on knees, with a look of happy expectation. All Joe Pender's wrinkles were set in a smile. But there were other faces, women's mostly, tight-lipped, with eyes that took in every thread of your dress and lingered on the only frayed one. With what relish Sara Lawry, for instance, the withered spinster credited with the least charitable tongue in Polverras, must be counting the minutes of delay – which would be multiplied when she recalled them tomorrow. I began to understand Ann's dread of her neighbours.

But now the vestry door opened, and the preacher stepped on to the platform.

She looked ridiculously young. Her grey dress was plain, her black hat severe. Her hands, when she clasped them in prayer on the reading-desk, appeared large and clumsy.

"Friends," she announced in a hesitating voice, "we will open our service tonight with the hymn 'Oh, pilgrim bound for the Heavenly land'…"

We sang heartily to a rollicking tune. But when we sat down, the atmosphere remained cool and appraising.

Still standing, Ann closed her eyes and began her extempore prayer. Its first sentences were stilted, slow. Then the words came quicker. Her eyes opened, restoring animation to her face. She raised them, she seemed to be speaking directly to God as to a personal friend, unseen, but listening and close at hand. Bit by bit, her English of the prize-winning Board School scholar took on the warmer Cornish accent, became interpolated with Cornish idioms.

She was praying for charitable judgement.

"Oh Lord," she said, "I reckon Thou must be fair mazed sometimes at the grossness and stupidity Thou seest all around Thee, here and everywhere. But Thy eyes can see through it to the striving towards Thee what lies beneath. Lend us sinners, I beseech Thee, Thy kindly eyes with which to look on one another."

Groans of assent broke from the congregation. Joe Pender, mopping his brow, uttered in his deepest tones three glib "Amen"s. I doubted his absolute sincerity – but there was no doubting John Peter's. Arms outflung, he sprang up, crying aloud: "Glory Hallelujah!" On his beaming face unexpected lines of sensitivity revealed themselves.

As Ann prayed on, groans and "Amen"s came faster. Eyes were shining. Criticism had died. I could sense a wave of fervour sweeping through the Celtic congregation, breaking down barriers of neighbourship, relationship, and petty enmities, uniting all in an ecstasy of unpent emotion.

This fervour lingered while Ann Praed read the lessons and while we sang more hymns.

On beginning her sermon, as on beginning her prayer, the girl was ill-at-ease. She dropped the bunch of notes she was carrying, looked at the Superintendent, and stammered with confusion when a boy picked up the scattered pages for her. But she warmed quickly to her subject.

She had chosen the text: 'If any man love Me, let him take up the cross and follow Me'. Her sermon was an appeal for mission work. But she made of it a bigger thing than that. She made it a passionate exhortation to spiritual service, which left no loophole for any shirker, which should have stirred the most sluggish. Her words flowed forth, unwavering. A sweep of her hand and the notes went flying off the desk again, but this time to lie unheeded. Her face was transfigured by a radiance centred in the eyes; those eyes which, I felt, no longer saw the stark walls, or the heavily-trimmed new hats, but which looked beyond to a whole world peopled with souls to be saved.

At the end of forty minutes, she sat down. The flush ebbed from her face, leaving it pale and dull. Leaning back, she asked in a tired voice: "Will one of our elder brothers now lead us in a prayer?"

Ezekiel Reynolds stood up.

His words, after the preacher's, sounded conventional and heavy. They framed thanks for those whose gifts fitted them for special service, and an appeal that full scope for these gifts should be given.

During the final hymn, the Superintendent exchanged whispers with the Reynoldses; and when Ann Praed rose and passed through the vestry door, he too rose, and followed her.

We left the chapel, once more all chattering, gossiping neighbours. I had meant to slip off at once, and leave the book I was lending on the doorstep of the Praeds' home; but the Treloweths and Joe Pender cornered me for a discussion of the sermon. Ten more minutes had passed before I turned towards my destination, up a lane to the left of the chapel.

Soon I heard hurrying steps behind me. They were Ann Praed's. She was looking happier than I had ever seen her before, or have seen her since.

"Miss Barton, I'm delighted that you should be almost the first to know! For it was you who said the other day that my opportunity was sure to come."

"Good news?"

"My chance *has* been sent. And I have taken it. The Superintendent said kind things about my preaching and promised to recommend me for a grant for special training at our College. That means I shall get away soon, quite soon. Everyone has been some kind: The Reynoldses have promised to see that Father gets a good woman in to mend and cook for him. And poor old Father, when it comes to the point, will never hinder what is for my good."

"You should be a great success," I said.

She answered with complete confidence: "Yes. I have been chosen, and I shall be given the strength to do my work."

We were nearing her home, the whitewashed cottage that stood back from the road, when we saw in a group Billy Richards, Glorermay, Billy Berriman, and the village policeman. Billy Berriman was leaning against the hedge. His motor-cycle lay in the ditch beside him, crumpled up, his suit was covered with dust, and blood trickled from a scratch across his putty-white face. The policeman was taking notes.

Ann and I stopped dead.

"Tedn't Mr Berriman's fault," Glorermay was urging. "Billy here and me what had just slipped off for a bit of a walk like, after chapel, seed it all. And Mr Berriman couldn't help en no-how, could ee, Billy?"

"Twasn't his doing," corroborated Billy Richards.

"Sure ee wasn't doing more than twenty miles an hour?" demanded the policeman of Billy Berriman.

"Dead certain I wasn't. Leastways, not all the way along turnpike from Belruth. Maybe as I did do a bit more coming down-hill here, seeing as how I durstn't keep a – a lady to Two Tinners waiting, the first time for a fortnight she's said she might let me take er riding."

"You'll be called upon to give evidence later."

"Aw now, but honest, Mr Higgins, a feller can't elp hitting a man what comes out sudden and dodges about the road like a darned old rabbit. Won't jail me – will ey?" concluded Billy Berriman through chattering teeth.

"Not when me, who knows the victim, has spoke to em," said the policeman. "Fair tight he was, by the smell of en. Well, I daresay three ribs and his game leg broke, and a busted head will teach William Praed *his* lesson."

"My father!" Ann sprang into the group.

"Yes, Miss, I was coming to warn ee he'd had an accident. Doctor's with him now."

She went into the cottage.

DURING the next week, the victim's condition was the talk of the village. – He was too ill to be moved to Belruth hospital. He was raving mad. It was concussion. Nonsense, he was to have both legs amputated. Mrs Treloweth knew for a fact that the doctor gave him only three days to live. And another fact was that Billy Berriman would be tried for manslaughter.

Daily I made enquiries at the cottage. But I was always met by one or other of the neighbours who took turns to give Annie a hand. Annie herself, they always told me, was sitting with her father, who must not be disturbed.

It was noon on the eighth day after the accident when I met Ann at her gate, taking leave of the doctor. I noticed the lines of fatigue in her face, the leadenness in her movements. She asked me in; and when we had sat down on each side of the parlour table, she hid her face in her hands and remained silent for a full minute.

Then: "Well, that is over," she said.

She raised her head and gazed at me as though from a great distance. "Excuse me, Miss Barton. But the doctor has just told me as a certainty what he warned me of as a possibility three days gone. Father is out of danger."

"What a relief for you!" I exclaimed conventionally.

Ann opened her lips, paused. Then she said emphatically, more to herself than to me: "Yes, I'm thankful. I am truly thankful." She continued: "He will be able to limp around after a while. But he will be very queer in the head, much queerer than before, Doctor says. And like a sick child, he will have to be looked after and not crossed."

"Still, if you get some reliable women to take care of him when you go away."

"It would have to be day and night and that much I can't pay for."

She said no more, but I understood. I leaned forward and took her hands in mine. "Something *must* turn up," I said.

My words sent a shudder through her. And the look that came into her face was of fear, downright fear.

A knock at the door heralded Glorermay, who was carrying an envelope.

"Letter from the Superintendent for ee, Annie," she announced. "Leaving Boskew today, he is, and he says will you let en have an answer by evening. But I can't wait to take en, for I've got saffron cake baking, and Mrs Reynolds' slab is that jumpy by this wind you can't trust en out of sight."

A cheerful grin, then Glorermay was gone.

Ann read the note and passed it to me.

The Superintendent offered to have William Praed placed in an institution for the sick. His note concluded: 'Rest assured, dear fellow-worker, that my recommendation and that of our friend Ezekiel Reynolds will ensure your father's admittance, and that every care will be taken for his physical and moral well-being. In view of his present mental condition, the decision rests with you. But I urge you to consider the debt of service that those endowed with special gifts owe to the Ministry.'

"What will you answer?"

The girl looked at me strangely, and uttered a sound that was almost a laugh. "I – I put my hand to the plough when I started preaching. Didn't I? Didn't I, Miss Barton? And those who put their hands to the plough must not look back."

A grumbling call came from above.

"Ann, Ann-ie. Blarst it, where be the little maid to?"

"Come and see Father," she proposed in a changed tone. "We put him in my room, because it's the sunniest."

We went upstairs to a room sparsely furnished and neat to bareness, its whitewashed walls decorated only with coloured prints of Bible texts. The sick man lay in a truckle bed. His feverish eyes peered out from beneath bandages; he waved one arm in the direction of the text that hung above the bed's end.

"Annie, pitch out that there pious muck," he demanded. "And fetch me a pint to Two Tinners, there's a good little un."

"The doctor says you mustn't have beer."

He broke into a stream of oaths, which she checked by asking quietly: "Do my texts really worry you, Father?"

"Fair sicken me, they do. Pitch em out, and nail up they pictures what I bought in Marseilles, that's to my own room now."

Nerves evidently at breaking point, she snapped out: "I'll not have the disgusting things in any room I come into. – I'll – I'll burn them as soon as he goes away, Miss Barton. Now, lie quiet, Father."

She crossed over to the bed. The sick man caught her hand in his, pulling her towards him.

"Annie, me dear," I heard him mumble, "don't mind yer old Dad if he is teasy. Blarst me if there isn't but one thing I couldn't bear – not to have ee staying along of me."

I left them and went quietly back to the parlour.

TWENTY MINUTES passed before Ann came down. Her step was quick and firm. Under her arm she carried the framed texts, and in one hand she held out a sheet of notepaper.

"Miss Barton," she asked, "would you be so kind as to leave this at Boskew for the Superintendent? And read it first, please. I – I can't seem to think clear just now. And I want to refuse his offer politely but definitely."

I looked at her face. Those last twenty minutes seemed to have stamped on it sudden maturity.

"Poor Miss Praed!" I said. "But do you think you have made the right decision?"

"Think! I know it. That was just the trouble, Miss Barton. I knew all along which choice I ought to make. Now I have made it, I'll be feeling all right soon."

She tried to smile.

4

A WOMAN OF FORESIGHT

"MRS BOSKEW REYNOLDS must have took ee for a real lady, my dear," opined Mrs Treloweth, while counting the eggs she had brought me for pickling. "Glorermay says as she's bidden en wear her white apron and serve ee tay to the front parlour. Tisn't many as Mrs Reynolds does that much for."

"She looks a proud woman."

"And proud she is. It don't do to put Martha Reynolds in mind of how she had to help pitch muck and dig tateys to her father's farm, they was that poor. She's done justice to Boskew House, though, these twenty years since she married en. But between we, Miss Barton, they Guernseys that Mr Reynolds leaves her take charge of is now even dearer to her than her back parlour. If ee wants her to take ee to her heart, make out as ee's fair daft on pedigree cows."

Thus forewarned, I set out that afternoon, across the moor, to call on my landlord's wife.

The farm-house stood in a suntrap, sheltered by a hill to the north, and overlooking meadows that sloped gently to the cliff-edge. Yet it always struck me as cold and forbidding. Its pebble-dashed walls stared, its glass porch aggressively red-white-and-blue. A wide concrete path round its base kept at bay all growing things, and a high concrete wall surrounded the front garden with its two squares of lawn, each decorated with a stunted palm, a clump of pampas grass, and a concrete-edged bed containing six geraniums. A stile and a gate gave entrance.

I climbed the stile, and found Ezekiel Reynolds waiting with outstretched hands on the further side.

"Some pleased I am – I'm delighted to see you, Miss Barton."

He took my arm to help me over, kept it within his a second

longer than necessary, and then dropped it so abruptly that I looked up.

Mrs Reynolds was opening the porch door.

"Come in, Miss Barton, and make yourself at home," she greeted me. "We don't stand on no ceremony here."

"Bluff and simple and hearty, take us as you find us. – I was wondering, Miss Barton, if you would like to see the tater-plants from our prize seed afore you take your coat off."

"Or wouldn't you rather I showed you the cow-sheds, Miss Barton?"

Both were smiling. But detecting a tartness in my hostess's tone, I said I would see the cow-sheds first.

Ezekiel Reynolds accompanied us through the hall, and into the kitchen where the brasswork on a slab twice as big as mine winked back at copper saucepans on the walls.

There, Mrs Reynolds stopped short and called: "Glorermay!"

Glorermay hurried out of the pantry.

"Didn't I tell you to scrub this floor?"

"Ess, M'am. And I done en."

"Would you like to be judged according to a floor with they three stains left on it?"

"No-o, M'am."

Mrs Reynolds turned to me. "There's many," she explained, "as judges a housewife by her dishcloths. But *I* says, judge her by her floors. She can hang new dishcloths on the line and keep the dirty ones hid away from her neighbours. But there's no deceiving possible with kitchen floors."

"Aye, Mrs Reynolds always has been a great one for floors," chuckled the farmer. "Why, I recollect how, before we married, I even caught her scrubbing one herself on a Sunday."

"*I* hold that Church or Chapel-going don't do you much good if you're content to come back from it to a dirty kitchen. And as for Sabbath-breaking, I mind hearing, Ezekiel, how your father once thrashed you for sneaking off magpie-shooting instead of to evening service. – Now, Glorermay, scrub that floor again. It will keep you a bit late, but you owe me them ten minutes you spent gossiping with Billy Richards at lunch time."

"Ess, Ma'm."

"And tell me the minute Billy and John Peter fetches back that crate from the station. They're late. Don't you dare forget to tell me, now."

She spoke sharply, yet once outside the kitchen, she said: "Good little worker, Glorermay is. And trustworthy. But it wouldn't do to let her get conceited."

From one paved yard we passed into a second, round three sides of which ran stone cow-houses. Mrs Reynolds lifted the latch of the nearest door.

"I'm going to show you the finest Guernseys in Cornwall, Miss Barton. That's what three years' keen buying and careful breeding have made Boskew herd. Afore I'm laid out for burying, I'll see the richest stock fanciers in Britain sending their beasts to stud here."

She paused and looked behind her. Her husband had gone.

Then she continued: "Pedigree stock-breeding needs brains and organizing powers. Good judging of human nature too, since you deal with men through cows. Many say that it's a man's job, that a woman's powers stop at her back door. Do *you* think so too, Miss Barton?"

"I believe a woman like you can succeed in anything she sets her mind to."

"Then you and I can get along together. Especially as I fancy you won't misunderstand my words, as many of the neighbours do. Life's been no easy job for me, Miss Barton. Eighteen years of my married life gone before I could try my abilities beyond the house. And then this lameness coming after my youngest was born. But I've found the means to beat that obstacle too. Today, soon as the men come back from turnpike, I'll show em all as I've got it beat. – Here are the milkers."

In the long shed the sunlight, filtering through barred shutters, glinted onto clean straw and dappled the sleek, finely proportioned beasts that stood chewing their cud or nuzzling fodder. The scent of hay, the animals' breaths and the not unpleasant odour of freshly dropped dung mingled in a pungent sweetness. Mrs Reynolds moved from stall to stall, stopping here to smack a rounded flank, there to pat a muzzle, or run her hand caressingly over a well-filled udder.

"This is Cherry, daughter to my Royal Cornwall winner. There's teats for you – fair dripping, they're that full. But mark my words, Miss Barton, it's Butterfly here that will make my best milker when she calves come Michaelmas. And her calf by Cambridge King will be worth more than fifty acres in brocoli. Yet there's farmers who says good ground is wasted on pedigree cattle. I says, they stick to their grandfathers' farming mostly because brocoli and taters don't need meating late at night, nor sitting up with when disease strikes em."

She was speaking eagerly. A flush coloured her lined cheeks and her lips had lost their droop. I could believe now the report that she was only forty-three, and in girlhood had been beautiful.

Then her face hardened again. She stopped before some heifers who were munching their hay more greedily than the others. Taking the nearest one by the horn, she drew its head towards her, and, with finger and thumb, pulled back an eyelid. The inner rim was almost white.

"Bloodless. Been left too long on poor pastures, they heifers have. That's what comes of the cattle being minded out of my sight, of my being able to hop around no farther than a cat fresh out of a gin. But there'll be a change soon, Miss Barton – soon as they men get back from turnpike. And when Boskew Herd is worth thousands, you'll see how all Polverras will come running up at the crook of my little finger."

The tea-gong broke in on her speech.

"Don't hardly know why I'm chattering on so, Miss Barton. To speak truth, I'm feeling a bit beyond myself today. I don't want it thought that I'm anything but a good farmer's wife doing her best by the work her husband trusts her with. Ezekiel's heart being weak, it's only right I should help him with his burdens."

TEA in the front parlour was not a cheerful meal. Purple wallpaper gave the room a funereal air, which was heightened by the large photograph of a tombstone hanging above the piano, between life-size portraits of the Reynoldses. My hostess fidgeted, and kept looking at the clock, while talking of potato disease, the latest deaths in the district, and the difficulty of finding farmhands whose idea of a fair week's work for thirty shillings matched her own. Not until Glorermay had cleared away, and Ezekiel had come in and drawn his armchair close to mine, did she mention cattle again. Then she said:

"Now Miss Barton, tell Mr Reynolds how you like Boskew Guernseys."

"They are splendid beasts."

"Tidy-looking, they are," agreed Ezekiel jovially. "And praise be, we can afford a few fancy cattle so long as there's the profits from brocoli and taters to pay for our daily bread."

"It's high-priced breeding stock, not brocoli and taters, that'll butter the bread of the future. Only some stick-in-the-muds won't use their eyes to see that."

Reynolds flushed. "I reckon you and I, Martha, can leave worrying about the bread of the future to them as has children to eat it. – Seen our stone, have you, Miss Barton?" He pointed to the picture of the tombstone. "It's to the Wesleyan half of the burying ground. Well, well;" he thumped his chest; "I was sound as a young man, heart and all. There's no weakness on the father's side to reproach for the fact that our seven little ones lie there."

Mrs Reynolds answered sharply, as one flinging back a challenge: "Seven born in six years. More than any sane farmer would ask of a cow."

An awkward silence followed.

The farmer broke it by coughing and saying: "It seems one may mistake the will of Providence. It was a favourite conviction of mine that when I grew old I'd lead my children to hear the Word."

To change a conversation in which both host and hostess were clearly angling from opposite sides for my pity, I said at random: "You are certainly clever at amusing children, Mr Reynolds. I've watched you set the little Treloweth girl hunting for sweets in your pocket."

"Oh! Give Winnie Lizzie sweets, do you?" asked Mrs Reynolds.

"Well, Martha, you and I agreed to have a neighbourly care for the innocent child."

"To help with clothes and money, yes. But it don't look too good for a man of your public reputation to go dandling a child of sin."

"What do you mean? Everybody knows whose child Winnie Lizzie is."

"Do they? Sometimes I think I do, and if I ever make sure – "

Whom could Martha Reynolds threaten thus? For a threat this was.

But she left it incomplete; and just then the door opened, and Glorermay announced: "Billy and John Peter is back, M'am."

Her mistress rose, smiling.

IN THE KITCHEN we found Billy Richards, John Peter, and Joe Pender standing besides a large crate.

"What's the little surprise we have here, Martha?" asked Reynolds.

"That's what all they we met along turnpike been axing," said Joe Pender. "Harry Jago, when he sees tis for Boskew, he guesses 'Tis a perambulator.' Queer fancies that boy has! But I says, 'More like tis a second piano, to look matey with the one they has already'."

"Put the hammer and chisel to it, Billy," ordered Mrs Reynolds.

The lad worked for five minutes. Then he pushed out of the crate an invalid's chair with a motor attachment.

There was a general gasp of surprise.

Mrs Reynolds laid both her hands on the chair's back, letting her crutches clatter to the ground.

"Here's what will break my tether. No more being limited by they there sticks." She kicked the crutches. "From now on I'll be getting around with the best of you. – What are you all gaping for?"

"But, Martha, I never grudge you the car for getting around in."

"The car won't pass along narrow farm tracks. This chair will take me near to every meadow in Boskew, so as I can see that the Guernseys are as well minded to pasture as to the cow-yard.

There'll be no more leaving heifers go poor on ground what's et bare; no more work skimped because I can't keep an eye on it."

Billy Richard's face was blank. John Peter's and Glorermay's expressed humble admiration.

Ezekiel Reynolds looked vexed. "But Martha, they rough tracks would shake an invalid like you up something awful," he protested.

"It'll take but four men's work for two days to level the lot of them proper."

"And they young bulls that are waiting to be sold are that treacherous. I'd not have a minute's peace for thinking as one might corner you, all alone – "

"Let him. I've yet to meet the man or beast as I can't put the fear of the Lord in."

Then, this here mechanism – I doubt a woman could handle it proper."

"You needn't fret over that, Ezekiel. I took lessons when I ordered the chair, to Belruth that day when you went on alone to a Rechabite meeting. See for yourselves whether I've mastered it."

Mrs Reynolds seated herself in the vehicle. There was a buzz as she started up the motor, then she rode dextrously through the back kitchen and into the yard. John Peter followed them slowly.

Billy Richards looked his employer full in the face. "Keeping it, is she?"

"Reckon she is, boy. When the Missis is set on a thing. – Well, it's a principle with me to indulge the weaker vessel."

"Then I'd best give ee my week's notice now, Mr Reynolds."

"What, leaving me!"

"Mr Eva to Trelease has promised to take me on any time as I was free."

"Not satisfied with your wages, ain't you? Think it over, boy. As a matter of fact, I've been thinking of raising you two shillings a week soon."

"Thank you, Mr Reynolds. But I'm one as wouldn't stand being chivvied in my work, no, not for a pound extra. I'll leave on Saturday. Evening to ee."

And he walked out.

Reynolds passed a hand across his brow. "Such vexations don't do no good to my heart. Praise be, Andrewartha, Robin Willy, and Tom Laity isn't all that independent. But there's no telling where the stir a woman's whim starts will end. I feel this is almost a matter to ask Guidance on."

Joe Pender remarked dryly: "A husband what holds the purse-strings needn't wait for no guidance to send back goods ordered without his consent."

"If he holds the purse-strings – " Then, checking himself, Reynolds started anew: "It don't do for a man who is standing for County Councillor to get a name for being hard on his wife. Sets the women's votes against him."

"True enough, Mr Reynolds." Pender was watching him closely. "But many a trial can be come over, if you set about it right. Paul Skewers, now, when his sister went daft about having a motor, was terrible against her gadding around in place of staying home to keep house for en. But he bought and paid for a motor-car. And between we, twas mostly the praise Jane Skewers gave her brother's openhandedness as got him voted onto the School Board. Yet would ee believe en, after the election the car wouldn't run proper, no, not though Paul tended en with his own hands. Always a tyre leaking there was, or a spring bust, and the screws seemed to fair tumble out of en. Not dangerous things, but they was always happening. And when the motor had spent the best part of a year in and out o Belruth repair shops, Jane was that sick of en she got Paul to sell en. Paul, ee says to me private: 'Tis remarkable how a trial don't last unbearable long if you knows how to handle en'."

Reynolds had listened with twinkling eyes: now he burst out laughing. "Well, Pender, I hope the Missis's chair don't have no breakdowns, for I can't bear to see a sufferer like her crossed in her whims. But that mechanism don't look too strong to me. – Hey, John Peter, how's Mrs Reynolds getting on with the new toy?"

John Peter had re-entered the kitchen. "Fair c-charging back like a t-tractor, ee be. L-look at en."

I went into the yard. Reynolds followed, and when his wife halted the chair, he put his arm tenderly around her shoulders and helped her out.

"Looking better for the run already, you are, Martha. I doubted you'd have the strength to use that contraption, but seeing as you have, we'll call it my birthday gift to you."

She stared at him hard, then nodded. "Thank you, Ezekiel." And as she picked up her crutches she muttered: "It do look fittier for you to have the credit."

John Peter was walking round and round the chair, without daring to touch it. "Mr R-Reynolds, I'd dearly l-love for my M-Missis to set eyes on this here chariot."

"Bring her, Treloweth. And anyone else who cares to step along. When not in use, you'll find the chair in the garage, which is never locked. The best place, eh, Martha? Handy for I and the men to keep it oiled and in good running order."

His wife turned round sharply.

"Think I'm going to let you and the men have the worry of my chair? And you all that busy with the taters. I've got the spare stall in the second cow-shed boarded up ready for it, and a padlock on; and a girl can do all the tending it needs. – Glorermay!"

"Yes, M'am?"

"You'll clean that chair and shine it up proper every morning. You'll take it out and put it back when I tell you. You'll keep the spare key to the padlock. And if I catch you letting anyone else put a finger to what's to be your job, out you go packing. That's clear, ain't it? Here's the key."

She turned to her husband with a smile that said: 'Out-manoeuvred!'

5

SALVAGE

THEY all gave me warning.

At noon, Mrs. Treloweth took in her still-wet sheets from the bushes on which she usually left them to bleach for a day and a night.

"I don't want to come back late from Belruth market and find em one-half round chimney and tother half to rocks down Cove," she explained.

John Peter spent most of his lunch-hour criss-crossing his henhouse roof with thick ropes weighted with stones, as if it were winter and gales were due.

Glorermay told me that the cows, after running about with their tails in the air – sign of wind—had lain down, "each to keep her bed dry against the storm."

And on the cliff-path I met Joe Pender hauling his boat up high and dry, from the cove. He pointed to the horizon.

"Tis that clear, and after a Saturday moon. And they sea-gulls been laughing deep down in their chests. Signs of dirty weather."

A storm coming! Absurd to think of it on such a day, the last of a perfect month. The bay shone like a silver shield, patterned by dark currents; wavelets uncoiled themselves foamless, almost soundless, upon the shingle. The cliffs exhaled a scent of thyme and flowers, and the air was so limpid that every bush and hummock stood out, clear-cut. The birds, even the perky stone-chats, as if indolent with heat, seemed heavier than usual in their flight; the spiders and sun-beetles, slower moving.

Suddenly black clouds rolled up westward and blotted out the evening sun. A green light filtered through them. A breeze sprang up, swelled, and raised catspaws in the bay; the voice of the ebb-tide deepened.

Yet I went to sleep expecting only a strong wind and, perhaps, showers.

I WAS AWAKENED by one short, tearing, explosive sound. Soon after, a beam of light too strong and prolonged to be lightening shone full in at my bedroom window, then slowly swung away.

My bed was a-tremble. The ewer rattled in its basin, the mats flapped on the floor, the whole room seemed to be smitten with St Vitus' dance. The storm had come.

I went to the window and saw a searchlight, its pivot on the cliff-edge. Out to sea, a yellow flame shot up, flared, and died.

Within ten minutes, dressed in my thickest clothes, I had slammed the front door behind me. It took me longer to cross the hundred yards' length of my garden; staggering, blinded by rain, slipping in mud, thrice almost beaten to my knees by the force of the wind. Finally, losing my foothold altogether, I pitched forward, grabbed at the gate, which swung open, and then at the next object immediately in front of me, which proved to be the warm wet flank of a horse.

"Hurt are ee?" shouted John Peter's voice, while his hand grasped my arm.

Steadied by him, I leaned back against the foremost of three horses harnessed to a wagon, from which rose a rocket apparatus: – the searchlight on its pivot, a cannon-like machine on an iron tripod, buoys, and great coils of rope. On and around the wagon, their bodies contorted as they bent before the wind, moved a score of men wearing oilskins, sou'westers and sea boots. Looking along the searchlight's beam, I saw, lying some distance out in the bay, the decks and funnels of a small vessel tossing amidst huge waves.

"A wreck?" I yelled in John Peter's ear.

"Tisn't yet. Be un any minute," he yelled back.

A gust hurled my head-scarf into the darkness, whipped my hair across my eyes.

John Peter pulled me back. "Stand t-to shelter of the team, Miss. A-an wear this."

He pulled a sou'wester off his own head, and shoved it on to mine.

"But you need that yourself."

"D-don't matter. I be'nt of much importance, cept for holding they hosses."

Shouts were blown to us in fragments.

Joe Pender's voice: "...clumsy farm-hands, you. Leave me as is a seaman to fix the wind-gauge."

Harry Jago's: "She's sure drifting into Cove."

Others: "Looks like hand-steering's smashed."

"Life-boat's turned back to port...dursn't face that sea."

A second flare shot up from the vessel's deck. She was indeed drifting towards us.

"Make ready for the second rocket, boys," shouted Joe Pender from the wagon-top.

A roar, a shriek, and the rocket and its rope leapt out along the track of the searchlight.

"Missed again."

"Megaphone her, Uncle."

"They furrin Portugays won't understand."

An eddy of wind hit the wagon and sent the men on it reeling. The gale, which had seemed to be blowing all ways at once, suddenly rushed with full force south-west. The horses shivered; one flung up his head and neighed.

"Steady, good boy, steady," soothed John Peter. "Why, believe tis Mr Reynolds' car coming yonder."

Headlights shone down the lane, halted.

Ezekiel Reynolds strode into the group and his voice boomed out: "Safe is she, boys?"

"Drifting backwards straight for the Point, Sir."

"Us can't do nothing more for en."

"Ey say she's a-carrying of strong drink," John Peter told me. D-devil's end for a bad cargo."

"E've got the best eyes, Harry. What's she a-doing of?" Joe Pender roared to his lieutenant.

"Guess they're chucking her cargo overboard."

"If she gets past Pendu, current will land her safe on Treburthy sands."

Straining our eyes along the narrow path of light, we watched the ship reel to within what looked a mere stone's throw of the westward headland's black fangs. Ezekiel Reynolds climbed to the wagon-top and stood there, an imposing patriarchial figure, his bare head gleaming white.

He raised his right arm and pointed seawards. "Let us pray for em, Brothers. The Lord send her safe past they rocks!"

"Amen," muttered John Peter.

"Amen," echoed several others.

The ship lurched horizon-wards, suddenly described a wide curve, and swept out of sight beyond the headland.

"She's been saved, Brothers," bellowed Reynolds, climbing down from his vantage point.

"A good job too."

"Twill be Pendu rocket men's business to mind en now."

The tension relaxed. The men came crowding into the shelter of the wagon. "T-Tis something wonderful how your prayer was answered, Mr Reynolds," marvelled John Peter in an awed tone.

"Queer what tricks they searchlights play," remarked Joe Pender. "I'd have swore as she'd rounded that there point a full half minute afore Mr Reynolds opened his mouth."

Harry Jago picked up the megaphone and shouted into it so that not a word might be lost; "So that prayer was just a bit of fancy trimming, eh, Mr Reynolds?"

The taunted man turned on him, his light blue eyes protruding with rage. "This is no time for blaspheming, you son of Belial!"

Harry jerked his right fist upward, paused, drew back his lips in a dog-like snarl. Then he turned his back on us all and disappeared into the darkness.

Why such a graceless youth sometimes? I asked myself, a little irritated. Couldn't he give the benefit of the doubt, for once?

"Mr Reynolds, g-go up along, will ee?" invited John Peter placatingly. "The Missis 'll be proud to get ee a drop of something warm. And ee, Miss Barton, will ee tell en as I'll be coming soon as I got someone to t-take they horses and meat em and rub em down."

"I'll stand by for signalled news," said Joe Pender; "can't be long now, one way or tother, with this sea. Then I'll join ee."

The weather made even the short climb to the Treloweths' seem interminable. At last we were in the kitchen, where a fire was roaring, with a teapot ready on the hob. What delights! My selfish eagerness to partake of them, while that poor crew were still tossing between doom and survival, was cut short by a sudden stab of guilt. Perhaps the unspoken thoughts of my companions, steeped in inherited awe and respect for the sea, were affecting me. After peeling off our wettest top layer of clothing, we stood about in silence.

Tension broke when Joe Pender opened the door and proclaimed: "Poldhu team's got em off! Skipper and all. – Sitting down to tay and pasties at the Seamen's Refuge they'll be soon now, all they bloody Portugays."

"Thought their sort wasn't that set on tea, the poor souls."

"Mary Liza, believe me," – and the old sailor's tone, unusually serious, hinted at grim past experiences – "after a sousing like they've had, one ain't hardly human no more."

Mrs Treloweth started to pour out. "Anyhow, now we can enjoy ourselves good and proper. Reckon all here is teetotallers. Or ought to be – eh, Uncle?"

The fisherman was eyeing a half-open cupboard. "Looks like that black bottle might be some of your sloe gin, Mary Liza."

"Uncle! And you just saying…"

"*I* ain't been *in* the sea tonight."

Reynolds, who had accepted the best chair by the fire, spread his legs wider to the warmth and glanced up. "What? Keep sloe gin in the house, do you, Mrs Treloweth?"

"Well, Mr Reynolds, always been strict teetotal myself, I have. But I think us is mostly agreed there is nothing dangerous in sloe gin or port."

"Not in the port they sell in The Tinners," agreed Joe. "I drunk a pint at a swallow and didn't feel no different."

"But maybe Mr Reynolds don't hold with sloe gin even."

"Well, not as a habit, Mrs Treloweth. But seeing that this, like a wedding or a funeral, is an occasion of special need, I don't mind if I do take a drop."

Out came the bottle and Mrs Treloweth poured a meagre

measure of the liquor into each cup.

"Don't be scared of en, Mary Liza."

"'Tis terrible warming, Uncle Joe."

"I'm terrible cold. And Mr Reynolds must be fair exhausted after leading of us all in prayer. – Come'st on in, John Peter."

The latter was hanging his dripping oilskins in the passage. When he entered the kitchen, his long face looked pinched with cold, his hair trickled water and his trembling underlip was as purple as the hands he stretched out to the warmth.

"Fair daft as a May-gum ee looks, my dear," commented his wife.

"Poor chap is froze," sympathised Joe Pender. "A drop of your brew will warm en."

"Won't ee this once, John Peter?" Our hostess tilted the bottle above the empty cup.

"Ee kn-know I d-d-don't touch en." He pushed the bottle back.

"Come, come, Treloweth. As sure as I spoke on Temperance at Belruth last week, there's no harm in a drop of sloe gin once in a while."

"To refuse en is as good as saying Mr Reynolds himself ain't a good teetotaller", argued Joe Pender.

"M-meaning no offence to ee, Mr Reynolds, I can't. 'Tis the way I s-see my pledge."

"It's the one thing John Peter don't see eye to eye with me about," explained his wife. "*I* says, as we most all do, the pledge don't refer to sloe gin and port, what's like medicines."

Joe Pender seized the bottle, filled the cup nearly to its brim and pushed it under his friend's nose.

"Drink en up," he ordered.

Like a bewildered dog, John Peter stood blinking and peering from face to face. Surely he would yield, he who always seemed as wax in his wife's hands; he who repeated Ezekiel Reynolds' sayings as the loftiest of moral precepts! But no. He fled from his tempters.

"I-I'll take a p-pipe instead," he stuttered, and left the room. I heard him putting on his oilskins, then slamming the front door behind him.

"He'll be dry and all right in his sty," said Mrs Treloweth complacently.

"His sty?!" I exclaimed.

"The little old shed next to the pigs' house, where I do make him go to smoke. For I says he's as mucky as a pig with his old baccy. Tisn't but twice since we married that I've let en smoke a pipe indoors, and they was both times of great trouble."

"When Winnie left home, wasn't it?" asked Joe Pender.

"Ess," she answered tersely.

"Good news of Winnie, ave ee?"

"Er was well and to Plymouth still at Christmas when er last letter came."

Mrs Treloweth gave a jerk of her head in my direction. I interpreted it as a reminder to the company that they were treading on private ground, to which I was still too much of a foreigner to be admitted.

But the questioner continued, his eyes now on Mrs Treloweth's face, now on Reynolds': "Winnie Lizzie looks real smart in they clothes what Mr and Mrs Reynolds sent, don't she?"

"Ess. I don't know how we could keep en with us if twasn't for all they do for us and them letting us be a bit backward with the rent now and then."

"It was a charitable deed of yours to keep the child, Mrs Treloweth. And seeing it's only neighbourly to give a helping hand, I don't want nothing talked about it. – " Reynolds rose abruptly. "I'll be getting back home now, or Mrs Reynolds will be worrying. Good night all."

He went ahead to his car. Joe Pender and I left the cottage together, and as we passed the veronica hedge Harry Jago stepped out of its shadow.

"Uncle Joe, message has come through that all that boat's cargo had gone overboard before she reached Poldhu."

"There's luck! If this wind holds, currents will still be setting Roskennow way tomorrow – We'd best be down to Roskennow a bit before dawn."

"Mr Pender, I hope you're not leading Harry into any illegal practices!"

"Miss Barton, bless ee, I know the value of appearances, I do. If ee comes to Roskennow tomorrow, Miss, ee'll find Harry and me earning as honest a penny as ever I've done a-selling of my fish."

I HAD LEARNED to take mysteriousness in Joe's manner as a portent that something worth seeing was afoot; so next morning curiosity set my steps on the fieldpath to Roskennow Cove, a mile to the east.

The wind had ceased as suddenly as it had been born. A thick mist was muffling the sound of the waves and transforming the fields that I crossed into grey courts of mystery, the stone walls and stiles between which loomed up, large and spectral. I climbed the stile that gives on to the cart-track which leads to Roskennow, and jumped off its top step.

I landed beside a man's sprawling body. Stooping over it, I recognised the upturned face of Mr Crebo, our postman. He was dead drunk.

One of my most respected neighbours dead drunk in the ditch at half past nine in the morning – I rubbed my eyes –

By the side of the track was drawn up a line of farm wagons, handcarts and donkey jingles. A few yards below the stile, three farm labourers met and passed me, arms linked, bawling out a popular song.

The track steepens and passes through a cut in the cliff, to lose itself in the shingle of the beach. There, where the cliff walls form a majestic frame, I came face to face with Ezekiel Reynolds.

Whatever had happened to him? In his shirtsleeves, his eyes bloodshot, he was hopping from side to side, waving his arms.

"Praise, praise," he shouted. "Welcome, happy morning! Eh, eh, boys. Fast falls…"

"Mr Reynolds, please…" I was trying to dodge past him.

"Hullo, andsome young woman! Praise! It's safe, it's nothing but a weak kind o port."

I evaded his outstretched arm and ran on to the shingle, – and almost into the arms of Mrs Treloweth.

"My dear soul! Some pitiful, isn't en? I'm fair shamed you should see en like this."

"Is everybody tipsy today?"

"Tis all along of they old casks from the ship what are floating in. One came ashore leaking. And the fellows who had come down to earn a bit of salvage-money fetching of them in and taking em to Belruth, they sees the old busted cask marked 'Best Invalid Port'. And they takes en for a weak sort of port for the sick, weaker'n what they sell to Two Tinners."

"Why, it is probably three times as strong!" I exclaimed.

"That's what they learned after they'd drunk deep of en. And Mr Reynolds, ee drank along of other teetotallers, unsuspecting like. Come and see what's left of en."

She led me to where, on a bank of shingle, lay a large broken cask. One man sprawled across it, two others lay beside it sound asleep, the last crimson drops of the wine seeping into their clothes.

The small beach, shut in by sheer granite cliffs, was crowded with men, women, and children. Some stood peering through the mist out to sea; others talked in excited groups around casks and boxes and piles of miscellaneous jetsam. Two women were disputing the possession of a broken table. Children were sucking water-sodden oranges. A dozen men, carrying grappling-irons, billhooks and sticks, ran to and fro at the edge of the sea, copying the zig-zag progress of dark objects which here and there bobbed towards shore on the crests of grey-white waves.

Joe Pender stood resting besides three casks.

"Some handsome prize, aven't ee, Uncle Joe?" admired Mrs Treloweth.

"And ain't I deserved en, me as was down here watching since break of day?"

"Is that *all* you have salvaged in that time, Mr Pender?"

"Why, Miss Barton, what be ee a-thinking of? If there had been some more come in afore the coast-guards got wind of their coming, wouldn't they be piled up along o these here, like honest salvage?" And the old rascal looked me straight in the face.

"My John Peter don't seem to have got nothing yet."

"Hi, Uncle Joe," Harry Jago's voice rang out, "she's coming in."

I saw him break from a group by the waterside and wade

knee-deep into the surf. Joe Pender ran to join him.

A huge breaker, which sent the other salvagers scurrying inshore, broke over Harry's head, burying him in its cascade of foam. He struggled to his feet again, and, waist deep now, fought his way towards a cask which danced provokingly just out of reach. A throw of his grappling-iron, – he had the prey! From a wavecrest, it rushed down on him. He leaped to one side, and Joe Pender hooked it as it hurtled forward. Together, the two men started toilsomely to drag and roll it out of the backwash.

Just then, from the far end of the beach, John Peter came towards us, staggering under the weight of a large, lathe-topped wooden case.

"Oranges, as big as them what is twopence each to Belruth," he panted, dropping it at his wife's feet.

She gave the box one kick. Water oozed from all its joints. "Ee great bus, you! A pile o salvage pay we'll get for oranges what has the sea fair running out o them. Why didn't ee go in after one of they casks same as Uncle Joe's a-bringing of? – More o that port is't, Uncle?"

"Brandy, this one, I reckon," called Joe Pender.

He pushed his prize abreast of us, while Harry Jago ran back to scout again at the water's edge.

"A proper bit of money ee'll get, Uncle Joe, when they gives ee a third of what that fetches to salvage auction. And here's John Peter brought down the pony, and a donkey off the downs, all to hale off a lot o rotten oranges."

"Th-thought I done a good job, Mary Liza. Fair b-broke my b-back for en, I did."

"Tell ee what," Joe Pender offered. "As I and my partner haven't done too bad for ourselves, I'll give ee this here cask, John Peter."

"Th-thank ee, Joe Pender. But I w-wouldn't touch no b-barrel of drink."

"My dear life! Ee isn't axing ee to drink en," Mrs Treloweth pointed out. "Ee's helping ee to make an honest penny carting of it for them as aren't Abstainers to drink."

"Pledge don't mention carting of drink, particular, do it?"

enquired Joe.

"N-no. But d-don't look to me as its right to t-traffic in en."

"John Peter! to hearken to ee, anyone would think as when ee took the pledge ee clean forgot they marriage vows to support your wife proper."

John Peter scratched his head, baffled by this side-attack. "If ee makes it a q-question of m-marriage vows… But I'm terrible afraid it will bring a p-punishment."

"Now do ee talk sensible! I'll take the money when ee gets it. Go and fetch the cart to en."

"I'll be shamed for anyone to see me with en."

"So'll I, if ee goes to Belruth all mucky-like as ee is now. Take en home first, and shave and dress proper. Maybe Miss Barton will like a lift back."

The conscientious objector surrendered. In a few minutes, he and Joe Pender had hoisted the cask on to a small cart drawn by a donkey and a pony, and I had climbed up beside him on the narrow board which served as driver's seat.

As we toiled up the shingle, half-a-dozen of The Two Tinners's most constant patrons came hurrying onto the beach. They greeted us with envious derision: "Nothing left for us?"

"They blessed teetotallers as got the whole lot."

Further on, we came across Glorermay and Billy Richards vainly trying to shove Ezekiel Reynolds into his car. He was now becoming torpid, and every time they pushed him through the door he fell back again, limply. They stopped, panting and nonplussed.

Then Glorermay bent over him and yelled in his ear: "Twas Missis what sent us to fetch you, Master. *The Missis.*"

A gleam of comprehension came into the farmer's flushed face and without further resistance he allowed himself to be fitted into the back seat.

John Peter, looking back on them, shook his head. "That there shows as how t-traps is set for us in all drinks what isn't tay or water. – Comfortable, are ee, Miss?"

"Quite", I lied, clinging to my seat as we jolted over a rut. "Are you?"

"I'll never feel comfortable so long as I've got this a-back of me."

"But, Mr Treloweth, you are doing something that no one else here sees any harm in."

"T-tothers haven't made the same promise as me. I'll be p-punished, same as when I broke my f-first promise."

"What promise?" I asked, and immediately regretted the asking. For John Peter's usually sallow face was crimson and beaded with perspiration, and the reins were shaking in his hands.

He answered, looking away from me: "Me and Mary Liza had been married four years without getting any children. A-an we was fair set on h-having a little maid. Then our Winnie was born. And I th-thinks: What can I do to show the Lord as I'm grateful for en? And it comes to me, r-right while W-Winnie was being baptised, as I could best give up a bad habit. Took me t-time to find one. For I didn't swear. Didn't mind work, no more than I do now. D-did all my Missis axed, even to smoking my baccy in the sty. Took my g-glass of beer, I did, but in them days I didn't see no h-harm in en. Then it comes to me as how I was an awful complaining sort o chap, and when work w-was scarce and we couldn't have no butcher's m-meat, only fuggin and tater pastry, or a bit o sheep's lights for supper, I'd say: 'Tisn't just.' So I promised right in ch-chapel the next Sunday, – not out loud, you understand Miss – as I wouldn't c-complain of nothing no more. And things went fine the eighteen years I kept my p-promise."

"Well, I've never heard you complain of anything, Mr Treloweth."

"B-but I did, Miss Barton. When my Winnie left home."

"Suddenly?"

"Ess. Pretty sudden. And little Winnie Lizzie came, what we couldn't none of us hold up our heads about. An I – I was down to Two Tinners and they was all sympathising of me there, and a-handing of me beer. – And I says, out loud, I d-did: 'Mary Liza and me haven't done nothing to deserve this t-trouble. T-tis that there isn't no justice on earth nor from above.' Out loud I said en. And my punishment f-fell."

A minute's silence, then he went on: "F-from the very next day,

I got this here af-fliction in my speech and couldn't t-talk plain no
more, times when I got excited. Doctor, ee says twas the shock of
our t-trouble. But *I* knows twas my punishment."

"Is that why you gave up drinking?"

"Ess. For I sees as twas the d-drink that led t-to me breaking
my promise, and when I took the p-pledge, I promised to myself,
extry-like, not to take en nor touch en, not the port, nor the
sloe-g-gin, nor nothing. An not to make money by en neither.
And today I b-broke my p-promise."

The sentence ended in a groan.

"Don't worry, Mr Treloweth," I said, putting a hand on his
arm. "After all, you are getting the money for your wife, not for
yourself."

"Tis true. B-but I don't mind telling ee, Miss, I'll be some glad
t-to get safe back from B-Belruth."

MRS TRELOWETH had promised me a pasty of her own
baking. I went to fetch it that afternoon, and was waiting in the
kitchen for its crust to acquire that exact shade of brown which she
deems 'proper' when Ann Praed came to the door.

"Mrs Treloweth," she called out, "Mrs Tom Allen saw your
husband coming back home along the turnpike – and, I don't
want to upset you, but she says he was looking very queer."

"How queer?"

"Ill. Mrs Allen couldn't see much, as she was in the bus coming
back from the pictures, but she did say his black suit was looking
very queerly too. – I must get back to Father now – but I thought
you ought to know."

"Oh the great goky! His best black suit what he wears to
weddings and funerals. I might have knowed he'd chose that one if
I axed en to dress fitty! – Miss Barton, my dear, don't ee ever
marry a man what's too good a husband to complain on, but is that
simple ee can't even trust en to dress himself out of your sight."

Ann Praed had hardly gone when Joe Pender looked in.
"There's a painful surprise for ee coming down the lane, Mary
Liza," he announced.

"My John Peter – "

"Ess. Tis him. He don't seem exactly to know the road from the ditch. And – I wouldn't go accusing of such a Total Abstainer, but ee was smelling of brandy a cart's length off. I'm afraid, I'm terrible afraid he's broken the Pledge. Broken en proper."

And Joe disappeared in his turn.

"My John Peter took to drink! I'll never be able to look Polverras in the face no more."

"Come," I protested, "if he *is* drunk, it is your fault. You insisted on his carting the stuff."

"And wasn't it only because I believed I could trust him? Ee wasn't deceived by no label like poor Mr Reynolds was. And brandy, – brandy what none of my family has touched for generations. I'll learn him…"

Sounds in the yard sent Mrs Treloweth running out-doors. There was a minute's silence, followed by scuffles and protestations so loud that I went out to see what was happening. I found her wrestling with the door of the little stone hut, John Peter's sty.

"L-leave me be. L-leave me b-be," came in an almost inarticulate mumble from within.

Mrs Treloweth gave the door a final shove, and stretched her arm through the opening.

"L-let go my c-collar. Ee's a choking o me, Mary Liza!"

"Come on out will ee, and let me see the worst o ee!"

A pitiable figure stumbled headforemost through the door. The sight of John Peter dripping and exhausted after his night's work with the rocket was nothing to the spectacle he presented now. He wobbled as if he had hardly a bone in his body. He blinked. His best black suit hung in lank creases about him, and every crease exuded the smell of brandy. He swayed, then as a rabbit driven from one hole makes a bolt for the next, he lurched into the kitchen, where he collapsed half across the table.

"Oh, my dear life, his best suit which cost three pounds is fair ruined," lamented Mrs Treloweth, pulling the coat off his back and flinging it, with a gesture of fury, into the passage.

"I ain't d-drunk. I ain't d-drunk any," he babbled.

"Tell me that, would ee? Why, you're fair fuddled."

"Tis my punishment. Twas that there o-old cask."

"Where's ee to now?"

"Tis to a d-ditch down Carter's Lane."

"And what was ee doing with en in that there jolty old lane?" demanded the inquisitor, slapping his face with a towel wrung out in cold water.

"I f-felt some disgraced to be seen with en. And to turnpike, first I met a funeral and then I met the M-Minister, and he looked at me reproachful-like. And I couldn't face no more. Went down lane where tis quiet. And the c-cart jolted something awful, an the old cask rolled sudden and b-busted all over me."

"A proper waste!"

"Tisn't worst of en. I was a-slinking back, fair drowned. And I met Joe Pender. An I m-m-et a whole buddy of people up to turnpike, and I met the parson. And I met Minister himself again. An fair drowned I was. But I ain't drunk nothing."

"And who'll believe that, more's the pity?"

"No-not one of em. Tis that what's my punishment."

And John Peter, completely overcome, laid his head on the table and began to sob.

"Do ee believe ee hasn't drunk nothing, Miss Barton?"

"Yes."

"Well, I believe en too." The tone had softened. "Comes't on, old dear, if there isn't none others what believe ee, you and me'll just hold up our heads together, like we've had to do before. Come on, old sport." She patted his shoulder. "Put a good face on en."

"I reckon I'll go to sty and h-have a bit o baccy, tis comforting." John Peter, recovering himself, got up. "I – I'll face my punishment."

"Don't ee talk daft now. Tell ee what, my handsome, as tis a time o trouble, I'm not stopping at nothing to get ee back into good heart. Ee may have a pipe by the fire, provided ee don't scat they mucky ashes all abroad the floor."

6

CLARA CURNO STUDIES NATURE

'LUCKY I'm in no hurry this evening!' I thought, on finding two customers ahead of me in our West End Stores. Clara Curno, seated on an orange-box while waiting her turn, was dividing her glances between a shopping list, a boxful of ribbons and the store-room door. Sara Lawry's meagre elderly figure was stooped over the counter: she was sniffing at a choice of deodorising devices.

"This strong one," she decided. "It'll keep best and I'll only be hanging it at my back door of evenings, when Joe Pender's away on those there trips he keeps so close about."

"But why ever should there be bad smells then, my dear?" enquired Miss Williams.

Miss Lawry straightened herself and spoke resignedly. "I felt in my bones there'd be troubles, though I hadn't thought of that one! Too soft, as I told en, Joe was when he asked Harry Jago to come under his roof permanent – just because that fellow's unfortunate mother has gone to her last rest. – After all the long years Joe and I had lived as neighbours, peaceable – except for a cousinly tiff now and then – even though our back doors nearly touches! – But I mostly kept mine shut, of course."

"And now?"

"That Harry, on his own, is a shiftless cook, even for a man. Suppertimes, he'll forget the milk and leave it boil over, or the mackerel fry to cinders. Sicken me, mackerel do, anyhow. I was brought up more particular than most here and I thinks about how they gorges on drowned men. – So, you understand, when the cooking stinks come out of next-door's open door, they float in at mine."

"But if yours is shut – "

With a finger to her lips, Miss Lawry confided: "Twixt you and I, Miss Williams, I now feel obliged to leave my back door open, evenings, when Joe's away. I've no window in that wall. So, how else could I keep watch over what's going on in owner's absence? Might be girls, being lured in. Through the backyard way!"

When the amateur detective departed amid wafts of air-disinfectant, Clara Curno looked round alertly, and rose.

"This blue ain't quality enough for my hat, Miss Williams. – Ma says, a half of two-shilling tea, please."

Miss Williams steered her large body between the treacle barrel and the kipper box, drew a biscuit tin from below a shelf laden with kettles, tried her weight on it first with the left foot, then the right, finally mounted it cautiously, and lifted the tea-caddy from its place next to the mixed spice.

The tea wrapped, caddy and biscuit box replaced, she planted both hands on the counter and contemplated Clara's hat.

"And two pennyworth of mixed spice, please."

The spice was fetched.

"I'll look over they other ribbons while I'm here. – An ounce of black pepper, please."

"I'll see where's to. Never can remember till it sets me sneezing."

As Miss Williams ambled off, she nearly bumped into Billy Berriman who, in cricketing flannels, was hurrying out of the back storeroom. Clara's small hazel eyes brightened. She shook out the folds of her blue silk dress, and thrust forward one leg the better to display a high-heeled patent-leather shoe.

"Ullo," she drawled. "Didn't know there was a match on tonight."

"Aw, tis only a practice. I shouldn't by rights wear these brand-new flannels to en. But it gives the game a bad name if the fellow who may be next year's captain don't dress proper. Come to watch, will ee?"

"I've got lashings of things to take home to Ma."

"Leave your list here. *I'll* see ee gets service. Jimmy Wills shall take en round, seeing as I can't carry parcels myself in these ere togs."

"But Ma don't like me to hang around the cricket field alone, along of all they men. People talk so. If Miss Barton had been going – "

"I'll come," I said. "That walk will do as well as another."

Five minutes later, we were crossing the fields towards the cricket pitch. But we made slow progress, for Clara's high heels caught in the stiles, twisted in the ruts, and even when her escort's arm supported her, reduced her walk to a mincing hobble.

"If you'd got your bike mended, you could have taken me around by the road comfortable, Billy," she grumbled.

Billy Berriman gasped. "Not seen the front page of tonight's *Belruth Herald*, haven't you?"

"About the bargain sale to Madame Renée's, and next week's talkies?"

"And – and that bit o news to bottom right-hand corner, front page."

"I don't never bother with the news."

"But tis all about my riding licence being took away, to Belruth Police Court, along of William Praed making me knock him down."

"Bill Berriman! How long have they took it for?"

"Six whole months. Twasn't my fault, honest, Clara. Wouldn't stop to listen while I stated my case fully, they wouldn't – "

Clara jerked her arm away from his. "I've always known you was soft, Billy. But I never thought you was soft enough to let they old magistrates do ee down like that. And me counting on your bike to take me to *Flames of Youth* Wednesday."

"But I'll pay for ee by bus, Clara."

"Bus!" Clara snorted. "Along with a lot of old market women!"

"Don't ee look on the black side so quick. Think of the saving in petrol and repairs."

"Lot that interests me."

"It leaves a fellow that much more money to spend on going around."

"U-mm. It do that."

Clara allowed her arm to be taken again.

"I could afford to take ee to *Prairie Passions* tomorrow."

"I'll leave you know about coming, Billy. – Mrs Tom Allen did say Hugo Blakemore has a wonderful part in it as a strong man of Nature. A real man, Hugo is. Fair made me shiver down my spine, he did, the rough way he treated Lina Marzetti in that love-scene to *Queen of the Snows.*"

"You do change sudden, Clara. Why, last month you only fancied real gentlemen what wore top-hats like they'd been born in em."

Clara sighed pensively. "As a girl grows older, she comes to think less of men's clothes than of what's inside em. Harry Jago," she added, glancing up the field, "don't dress no better than they Breton fisher boys, but he does look manly."

My glance strayed after hers to where, a few yards from us, Harry was trimming the brambles that straggled over a stone wall. His rolled-up jersey sleeves revealed the play of muscles in his sunburned right arm as the billhook rose and fell. He had grown tougher, more uncouth-looking since his mother's recent death after a long illness. I was sorry never to have met her. She must have been a fine character, for clearly there was much good in her son, overlaid though it was by an acquired roughness.

While Billy Berriman and I answered his "Good evening" Clara Curno stared in the opposite direction. But once we had passed him, she looked back over her shoulder.

"I always feel awkward meeting that chap. Not fit for an honest girl to speak to, Ma says. Well, we all know one flesh-and-blood reason for Ma's way of thinking, doesn't us? And goodness knows how many bleeding hearts and broken bones may be marking its Dad's trail in the Wild West. – But I never likes hurting anyone's feelings. Puts me in mind of Hugo Blakemore, Harry do."

"Aw, he ain't that bad. Hugo Blakemore's sinews come fair busting through is clothes."

"Of course, Harry Jago's thinner. Gone thinner too, lately. I've heard tell how he don't even feed proper up at Uncle Joe's. Still, I could picture en pitching a girl on his shoulder in a sack, or saving her from lions – "

"Huh, I could be that sort of man of Nature if I wanted to," asserted Billy huffily. "Daresay I could lift ee in a tater sack, Clara."

"You'd be that scared you'd drop me at my first holler."

"As for lions, I ain't had no chance yet – "

"And dursn't take it if you had." Clara eyed him from his sleek head to his pipe-clayed shoes, then she tittered: "You a strong man of Nature! You! I bet you wouldn't even know how to catch yonder piggywidden."

She pointed to a very pink piglet with disproportionately short snout and long tail, who had just squeezed under the stile in front of us.

"Must have strayed from the field above the next."

"Then here's your chance of hunting," taunted Clara. "What's hindering you, Billy?"

"Don't want to muck up they flannels."

"Scared of piggywidden's biting ee, more like."

"Scared, am I? I'll show ee – "

He made a lunge at Piggywidden who, squealing, darted into the ditch. Another lunge and a scuffle followed, then Billy stood erect, holding Piggywidden by a hind leg and one ear.

"Ere's your old pig for ee," he crowed, trying to thrust Piggywidden into Clara's arms.

She jumped back. "Don't let the nasty mucky creature mess up my dress."

"But you axed for en."

"For you to put en to his mother. But maybe you dursn't that. His mother's big – "

"I wish she was a blessed hippopotomus to show ee – "

Billy Berriman led the way over the stile and into a turnip field. A triangular-shaped wedge of the Treloweths' field above projected into this one, near the stile, and a gap in this triangle's apex had been blocked up by an old iron bedstead, tied with string to two hawthorn trees. Against this bedstead a huge, mud-smeared sow was now hurling herself, while her furious grunts answered Piggywidden's calls for help.

Pulling the piglet's tail to make him squeal louder, Clara teased: "Poor piggywidden, poor piggywidden, wants to go to his gurt ugly Ma."

Billy advanced derisively, swinging his victim from side to side.

"Poor piggywidd – Oh, oh, mind; she's coming!"

A squealing of ten piglets scattered right and left, a crash of old iron and a snapping of branches, then the sow came charging through the gap.

Billy hastily dropped Piggywidden, pushed past Clara, and cleared the stile in two bounds. The next minute I myself had scrambled onto the turnip-field's stone wall, jumped, and landed deep among docks and brambles in the ditch.

The squeals had been succeeded by terrified human screams.

Billy was crouching on the safe side. But where was Clara? Judging from those yells, not far.

I peered over the wall.

She lay among the turnips. The sow bestrode her. Sharp cloven hooves were ripping up her blue silk dress, little bloodshot eyes were glaring down on her, powerful jaws, from whose yellow teeth foam dripped, were snapping only a few inches above her auburn curls.

The girl might be trampled and bitten to death –

"Billy, help!" I shouted, vainly trying to scale the wall.

There were running footsteps in the grass behind me. Then I saw Harry Jago dash past, over the stile and make straight for the sow, billhook in hand.

He struck her in the flank, and, as she lurched back, dropped on one knee between her and the girl. Squealing with rage and pain, she turned on her new tormentor. Again, and again, he struck out at her.

Clara still lay yelling.

"Run, you fool, run," shouted Harry.

Clara got up and tottered towards the stile.

The sow, who had momentarily retreated, charged again, snout low, eyes blazing. Before Harry could rise from his knee, she had bowled him clean over. She trampled across his body, and, jaws still snapping, ran to rejoin her piglets, who were cowering in the hedge.

From the stile came Clara's wail: "Oh, oh, I broke my ankle, busted my ribs – lost my shoe – "

Harry Jago picked himself up and went towards her, stopping

on his way to retrieve, from a rut, a shiny object.

"Here's your goldarned shoe," he said roughly. "Guess you're asking for trouble, playing the fool among turnips with they crazy high heels on."

"Better come along to my cottage, Clara, and we'll see what harm has been done," I proposed.

"I'm here to help ee along," encouraged Billy Berriman, who had rejoined us looking scared, but still spick-and-span.

"Leave me be, Billy Berriman! Mr Jago, if you wouldn't mind taking my arm. Oh – not that hard, it's that tender."

With Billy hovering in our rear, Harry Jago and I half-carried the girl to Chy Bgyhan.

"Wait outside," I suggested to the boys. "There may be need to fetch a doctor."

Once laid among cushions on my sitting-room sofa, Clara appeared to be fainting. However, cold water slapped on her face quickly brought her to, and while I undressed her, she uttered only a few moans.

"Fright, and four or five bruises, that's all," I said, refastening her dress after applying some lint and cold cream.

"Oh-h." Her tone was one of disappointment. "That beastly old sow. I'll see to it that John Peter sticks her tomorrow, I will."

A knock at the door set her leaning back again, eyes closed.

She opened them slowly on Billy Berriman. "Oh, its *you*, is it?"

"Feeling fit for me to see ee home, are ee, Clara? I'll take ee willing, seeing as I've missed the practice by waiting around. Not but what I'd miss a whole Final cheerful for you."

"You had the cheek to wait for me, you what ran when I was tripped up, and left me lying there to be gored to death, so as to save your own skin!"

"Twasn't my skin exactly, Clara. The thought struck me sudden as how that there sow would ruin my new flannels – "

"You darned stuck-up cowardly gucko, you. If ee don't get out this minute, I'll put ee out."

Forgetting her injuries, Clara swung stockinged feet to the floor. Billy went out swiftly.

When he had gone, the girl requested: "Would you kindly call

Mr Jago in, Miss Barton? That is, if you don't object to a chap as there's such tales about passing through your door."

"Village gossip means nothing to me."

"Why, you're like me then, Miss Barton. Broad-minded I am, really, only I daren't show it, Ma being so particular. So will you call him in, please."

I summoned Harry.

"Don't look much wrong with you now," he remarked, surveying the invalid.

"It's my nerves what don't show as is shook to pieces," explained Clara, looking pretty and helpless. "I'll never dare cross they fields alone. So I'll let ee give me an arm home, Mr Jago."

No response.

"Maybe I shouldn't ask no more of you, though, after all you've done already, saving my life," she continued more humbly.

"I won't take ee alone. You might faint and need undressing again or something," said Harry, suspiciously.

I volunteered to come too, and finally all three of us recrossed the fields, Clara leaning on Harry's right arm.

At sight of the sow, who now lay among the wreckage of the bedstead quietly suckling the piglets, she nestled closer to her rescuer. "The old brute fair terrified me. I never knew as pigs would take on that fierce about a bit of teasing."

"Reckon you ain't much acquainted with animals' ways."

"Ain't never had no chance to study them proper, Mr Jago. What with being cooped up helping in the house and bar so much, I leads an awful restricted life. I have to bottle up my cravings for getting to know Nature. Besides, farmyards are so mucky."

"The cliffs ain't mucky. You'd see plenty of Nature if ee walked there, free times, instead of running off to Belruth."

"But I haven't got no-one to go with. The other boys and girls think of nothing but dances and cricket and the pictures; they don't care about *real* things."

"Can't you go alone?"

"I blush to tell you, Mr Jago, but I'm that ignorant I wouldn't so much as recognise a fox till I fell over en. Not like you. I daresay you understands all animals from grizzly bears downwards."

"I take trouble to search em out. Found a pretty weasel's nest hidden away to Pendhu Point, yesterday, I did. With young ones in en."

"I'd dearly love to see that. Could – would you take me to it?"

"What! Come with me, would ee?" Harry Jago looked searchingly into the girl's face. The corners of his sensitive lips were twitching.

Clara dropped her eyes and answered demurely: "This evening's work has learned me better'n Ma could who is fit to go around with, and who ain't."

"Then – if ee'd really care to come, come. And welcome. Shall I meet ee by the gate next Miss Barton's cottage, seven o'clock Saturday?"

"Saturday – " Clara tapped a foot. "I'm not certain I could manage Saturday."

"Monday then?"

"Come around Friday and I'll leave ee know."

Harry stopped. "See here, Miss Curno, I'm not one to footch away time about being 'left know'. I've got to be answered now."

Wide-eyed, Clara gasped at him. "Lor! You're the first fellow what has spoke to me in that tone! I – I reckon I can come for certain Saturday."

"Come dresssed sensible. None of they high heels."

"I'll wear rubbers what hasn't no heels at all," she promised.

We were within sight of The Two Tinners and Clara announced she now felt strong enough to cover the remaining distance unaided. As we watched her walk away, Harry stretched out the arm which had supported her and touched it, wincing. There was dried blood on the sleeve.

"Reckon the old pig must have got her teeth into en when she sent me sprawling. Don't matter. I'll stick on one of Uncle Joe's Universal Cure Plasters."

"How could you endure that girl's weight on it?"

"Oh, I didn't mind that. Funny, I'd never have guessed as that doll was keen about things of nature."

"Perhaps Clara is 'misunderstood'."

Taking my words seriously, he said: "She and I've got that much in common, then."

"Why, who 'misunderstands' you?"

"Who misunderstands me? Oh ho! You can bet your boots, Miss Barton, that tomorrow the whole village will be ringing with how I knocked down Clara Curno and half-murdered the Treloweth sow."

"You wouldn't brood over gossip if you were less alone."

"What company is there while Uncle Joe's away to his sea-trips? Since I got back from Canada, folks has kept off me as if I had the scarlet fever, and it has got worse since Mother's. – Guess you've been told what I did at Mother's burying, Miss Barton."

"Ann Praed mentioned something."

"And spoke harsh of it? She too?"

"She only said it was a great pity."

"If her father hadn't plagued her into stopping home, if *she* had spoke the tribute to Mother, it would never have happened. I could have sat through *her* holding forth on the living cross Mother had to bear! – Meaning me. But when that greasy, cheating Butcher Vellanoweth started handing out that dope, I – I fair had to get up and walk out, Miss Barton, else I'd have struck him down from the pulpit. First time for more than three years I'd put my nose to church or chapel, and it'll be the last. They can keep their lousy Heaven; their Lord's kippering-factory would be good enough for me if twasn't I'd meet so many from Polverras roasting down there."

"People will soon forget."

"Not slighting their chapel, they won't. Those who, till now, have taken my word as I'd never done what's blamed on me, have now turned as dead against me as the rest."

His voice was bitter, and his black brows met in a scowl.

"Pull yourself together, Harry," I admonished. "If hard things are said, why, you must just live them down."

"And haven't I tried to? Never seen me tipsy, nor begging, nor fooling with girls, have ee? But what good has come of it? Not a straw-rick is fired, nor a crab stole from a store-pot, nor a girl got into trouble, this side of Belruth, but the whisper goes round:

'Looks like Harry Jago's games, that do.' I'm thinking I'd better start giving em cause for gossip, and have my fun for it. Guess I'll learn evil living easy enough, though I was raised to go straight."

"Not easily. For when your chance comes to do something really low or mean, your training, and your real nature will check you."

"Think that, do ee?" The words were half question, half sneer.

"Make a few friends, and you'll soon feel less disgruntled."

"Will I? – Well, I'll be having a bit of lady's' company come Saturday." He softened. "First time for three years I've took a girl out, Miss Barton. I've always reckoned Clara Curno a gad-about. But seems like there may be more qualities in en than folks have let her show."

"Then here's your opportunity to draw them to light," I encouraged.

For though mistrusting Clara's sudden love of nature, I thought her companionship would at least be better than none. The neighbours judged her: "Flighty, but with no real harm in her." Her chatter would be an antidote to Harry's moroseness; her dabbling in every local school-treat, social, or outing might draw him back into the circle of village life.

DURING the next few weeks, Harry obviously passed through a crisis. His appearance smartened; he was well-shaved, the elbows of his workday jersey were mended, with pathetically masculine darns, and his boots for the first time since his mother's death showed traces of polish.

He was still hedging in the fields near my cottage. On some days he whistled at his work; on others, he slashed away in silence, his lips and eyebrows set in gloomy lines.

Two Wednesday evenings running, I met him carrying the parcels Clara Curno had bought in Belruth.

The morning after that second meeting, Joe Pender called in, and met Harry, who had been to ask me the time, coming out. They passed each other without a word.

The fisherman pulled a live lobster from his bag, and laid it, kicking, on the table. "Ere's that big chap I promised ee, Miss

Barton. Left the boiling of en to ee, I have, seeing I've got to be off
again on the two o'clock tide, and Harry's argufying lost me
that-much time I couldn't get around to en last night. Eh well,
shows I'm getting stricken in years that I'd forgot a young chap
won't never take truth from a greybeard. Especially truth about
women."

"Young men say a great deal they don't mean."

"Ey do. But Harry's like a jelly what's been shook out too soon
and don't know which way to wobble. Three years running, he's
been off all young women because one gave him a shock; and that
though he's one of they poor creatures what can't get along proper
without a woman minding em. And now, the first tidy piece what
winks an eye at en, he fancies is winking for his soul's good. And
takes er out studying 'wild-life'. I reckon all that interests her in
wild-life is that when the furze is out of bloom, kissing's out of
season; and that the furze ain't never out of bloom!"

On the threshold he paused, turned back and said gravely: "If
there should ever be trouble while I'm gone fishing, I may call ee to
witness, Miss Barton, as I've tried to save a young fool from
himself."

THAT EVENING, when passing The Two Tinners at closing
time, I saw Harry Jago come out of the bar. His "Goodnight" was
thick, and his walk unsteady.

Early the next morning, he came to my door. "I've no more
hard jobs right now," he told me. "Shall I build ee a rockery,
Miss? Won't charge ee nothing for it."

His eyes begged me to say 'Yes'.

For the next three days, from nine o'clock till dusk, he delved,
forked, dragged up chunks of granite from the cove, and fetched
sackfuls of beautiful quartz from Wheal Glory, the disused tin
mine half a mile distant. He looked more sullen than ever. When I
praised his work, he hung his head and replied in gruff mono-
syllables.

The fourth afternoon, Clara Curno entered my garden.

How quickly the girl was maturing! In the last few weeks her
body had taken on ampler curves, her eyes more expression. Her

cheeks, softly pink as ragged robin petals, were free from their usual coating of powder. Harry Jago had once told me he hated to see powder on a woman's face.

"Harry Jago about, is he, please Miss Barton? I got something to tell him."

"There he is," I answered, pointing. "Just coming back from Wheal Glory."

Harry, stooping under his filled sack, was opening the lower garden gate. He glanced at Clara, then turned his back and slung down his sack besides the rockery.

"Mr Ja-go," the girl called.

There was no answer.

"Har-ry! Make a girl come running to ee, would ee?"

Dragging his feet, he came up the path.

"I just run around to ask if you'll be ready for our walk against six tomorrow, instead of against six-thirty."

"Are you telling me you're coming?"

"Why not?"

He shuffled and looked down. "After last Thursday – "

"Don't take on about that. Had to look like I was horrified, I did, because of Ma being there. But my goodness, I sees enough fellows take a drop too much ale in the bar not to fret about one more."

He glanced up sharply. "So that's how ee take it!"

"I mean to say – a girl as to suffer seeing and hearing an awful lot as she must shut her eyes and ears to. And she learns to look further'n all that. Six o'clock suit ee, will it?"

"It'll suit me fine."

Harry's shoulders were straight-set, and his step buoyant as he went back to work.

DURING most of the following day, clouds brooded overhead, and between clouds and countryside hung a veil of grey heat, palpitant, and shimmering, whenever a ray of sunshine pierced through to it, like a billion dragon-flies' wings. In late afternoon, the sun blazed out and the clouds withdrew beyond the hills.

There should be a magnificent sunset, crimson and mauve. The whim to capture some of its beauty seized me. Taking my long-neglected easel and sketching-block, I set out towards the spot that gives the best view of the western hills, the Watcher Crag, half way between Chy Byghan and Boskew. I followed the upper cliff-path, through fields of corn.

It was one of those rare voluptuously beautiful evenings. An electric vitality, born of the thunder-clouds, impregnated the hot air and seeped back from the hot, dry soil. Every living thing; reddening blackberries, mating butterflies, heather flowers open to the fertilizing bees, grain ripe almost to dropping; betokened fulfilment. In the stubble of the oat-fields, young cockerels, their crops bulging with hard new grain, bickered over yielding pullets. Uncut barley stirred and crooned, like a woman lazily awaiting satisfaction from her last, sadistic lover, the reaper.

The Watcher, one of a group of boulders which juts from the cliff fifty yards above its edge, is an upright block of granite large enough to hide three men. Below it, the ground breaks away into a dell which high furze-bushes gird on three sides; a dell where heather grows shin deep and where, in blossoming time, bees hum all day long.

I set my easel on a flat boulder immediately behind and screened by the Watcher, and started to work.

Suddenly, a whiff of cigarette-smoke reached me. Then I heard Clara Curno's voice: "Reckon I can smoke here without Ma getting wind of it. Show us your poor arm where the pig bit it, Harry. My stroking it don't hurt, do it?"

"'Tis soothing."

"'Tis a wonderful powerful arm. The very one you knocked down Mr Boskew Reynolds with afore you went to Canada, ain't it?"

"It be."

"Did he bleed much?"

"From the nose."

"You was pretty desperate that day, eh?"

"I was drove to it, Clara. I could have stood his pushing me back from the stile. But no fellow with guts in en could have stood the foul words he flung at me."

"Always thought myself, I did, that Mr Reynolds should keep his reproaching for chapel. Tisn't gentlemanly of a man to poke his nose into another chap's private affairs."

"Twas worse than ungentlemanly to set the whole village condemning me."

"Not the whole village, Harry." Clara's purring voice drifted up. "Not me. Never did I condemn ee, not in my secret heart I didn't, not when I heard all they tales. Not for robbing Jim Silas's lobster-pots, nor for firing the rick to Trelease, nor for the shooting and wounding they ses ee was sent back from Canada for."

"Gee! You been respecting me all along, and I never knowed it!"

"Think modern, I do. I'd never be unkind to a fellow like you just because he ain't the marrying sort, you know, Harry."

"But I never have harmed no girl, Clara. Never."

"Ee don't need to keep up pretences with me."

"But Clara, I never did one of they things that are blamed on me. Not one of em. Ee do believe as I've lived straight, don't ee, Clara? Ee must believe en. I – I'll swear it to ee on my mother's memory."

"All right, all right, don't take on. I don't mind what you like to make out. Look, Harry, how my shoulder what the pig hurt is getting all white again – "

There was a passage of indistinct murmering. Then I heard Clara say in sultry tones: "Go on, Harry, do it... Be a man..."

I rose, determined to go, whether the girl was shamed or not. And just as I did so, an animal cry rang out from a furze thicket. Then another. Cries of pain and terror.

"Hearken! A rabbit in a gin. – Clara, I got to go and knock en on the head."

"Leave en be."

"Ee's suffering!"

"That don't hurt us."

"I tell ee, I got to go. Mother brought me up not to leave rabbits suffering. Leave go my arm, you little bitch, you."

Harry, with the girl half-undressed, clinging to him, burst out from the dell. He forced off her hands, held her for a moment at arm's length, then pushed her back into the furze. White-faced, he turned in the direction of the rabbit's screams.

"You cad. No man after all, you ain't. I'll learn you. I'll tell the whole village how you tried to throw me over cliff when I struggled gainst ee…"

"Tell em then, and go to Hell and the village with ee," shouted back Harry as he ran.

Clara stood for a few moments tidying herself up and then made her way off.

Botheration! Thoroughly embarrassed, cross with the two young hot-bloods and with my own share in their *affaire*, I folded up my easel with a bang, and left the Watcher to the failing light.

7

FLOWER SERVICE

I HAD PROMISED the Treloweths that I would make sure of a front seat, from which to watch the children's Harvest Thank-offering procession. But, cajoled by autumn afternoon sunshine and a salt-savoured breeze, I was still dawdling outside the chapel porch when my neighbours arrived.

Winnie Lizzie was jigging up and down between her grand-parents. Mrs Treloweth carried a basket in which dahlias and Michaelmas daisies made a nest for two oranges, an apple, a jar of honey and six big brown eggs.

Her face was beaming as she asked: "Do ee like Winnie Lizzie's first Flower Service basket, Miss Barton? I even bought dahlias off Jim Silas so she should have real flowers, none of they honey-suckles and wild muck that some of the children make do with. Tonight, when the offerings are auctioned to help Chapel funds, us'll buy en back, to show our Winnie – if she ever comes home to see en. That's why I've decked it up so, with that W.L. and the date worked in red wool."

"Tis too showy," objected her husband. "Folks will be calling us p-proud."

"Isn't nothing wrong in the pride of having made a good job out of a bad one. What if spiteful tongues like Sara Lawry's do say that a love-child ain't fit to take part in a Flower Service? We'll make em own that Winnie Lizzie is as clean and fitty and well-mannered as any there, bless en. Almost like our Winnie was at her first Flower Service, ain't she?"

"Not so d-docile," said John Peter, gently resisting the child's efforts to wriggle her hand out of his as she demanded: "Let me carry my eggs, Granny."

"Ee shall later, my handsome."

"Now, now. They're *my* eggs, Granny."

"Even if your own pet hen did lay em, they ain't yours no longer now you've promised em to the Lord."

"Haven't promised no Lord – I want – "

"Put a peace on it. Look how proper all the little Allens are behaving."

Shepherded by Glorermay, who clasped in her arms an enormous vegetable marrow, the Allen flock of five boys and three girls were trooping towards us. Each child held a small basket of fruit and flowers; all were so clean and spruce that Winnie Lizzie stared at them as if hardly able to recognise her playmates.

At last her gaze lighted on four-year-old Tommy, on whose velvet suit – token that this cherub, at least, still indulged in sniffles, – was pinned a large handkerchief; and she gurgled: "Ou-h, cherries in Tommy's basket. Want to walk with Tommy."

"Glorermay shall take you in the procession, next to him, if ee behave. And us'll buy his cherries tonight. – Your Ma's doing herself proud, Glorermay, sending cherries at one-and-four a pound."

"They cherries have run me terrible short of money. Ma said she couldn't afford gifts as well as the Pictures tomorrow, and by the time I'd brought her round to it by promising to pay half, all Miss Williams' cheap apples was bought up. It's lucky that only Dutch auctions, with prices going down instead of up, be allowed in Chapel. I'll ask Billy Berriman to start this marrow no higher than eighteen pence."

"'Tis one of the R-Reynoldses' marrows, surely," said John Peter.

"Ess, but I'm bidding for en. Miss Barton, will ee do me a great favour; sit bang in front of it, to the front left-hand pew besides Mrs Reynolds? And stick your feet out and drape it a bit with your skirt, so that it would be bad manners for the Missis to go rolling it over. There's marks on it I don't want her to notice."

Hugging the marrow to her bosom, she hurried on in front of us.

Within, what magic the spirit of Harvest had wrought! With the fruits of garden and field, warmth and vitality had entered the usually severe-looking building. One could fancy that the jolly Nature-gods of pagan days had risen up and rollicked in, to tickle austere young Nonconformity and set a carnival wreath on her brow. Dahlias, Michaelmas daisies, and sheaves of corn were plumes of colour against the walls; greenery draped the hat-stand, the swinging lamps. On top of the harmonium stood vases crammed with marigolds and lupins, around its base and that of the reading-lamp, pyramids of apples, tomatoes, and oranges shared honours with carrots and swedes; here and there were basins filled with amber-brown hens' eggs, and one of ducks' eggs, opaquely pearl and green. The communion table was flanked on the right by a pumpkin, on the left by that monumental harvest loaf which, between August and October, travels from one Chapel festival to the next. But the table top had been left bare, to receive the children's offerings.

Children were in every pew; the youngest wedged between parents who thwarted the raids that small, covetous fingers attempted on baskets of fruit, the older ones in clusters, sitting still and erect. Even the small boys, awed by being actors-in-chief today, were refraining from munching peanuts and shying paper pellets.

"Glorermay has a good eye for effect." Mrs Reynolds' voice cut short my reflections as, helped in by her husband, she took her seat besides me. "Our marrow shows up well where she's put it to – there, just near you, Miss Barton. But the girl's getting too big for her boots. Because she'd tilled they marrows, and stayed late after work to catch the slugs, I'd promised to sell her one cheap; and she asked to buy this one off me. This one and no other. The idea of the preacher's servant taking the preacher's biggest marrow!"

"I myself was glad to let her have it," said Ezekiel. "This service is such a joyful occasion to me, Miss Barton, that I want others to enjoy it too. When the children hand over their little gifts at the Lord's Table, I shall feel for a minute as if I was a father myself."

"If you're so keen on it, Ezekiel, why haven't you ever taken Flower Service before?"

"I left a few years to heal my feelings, Martha. It would have been painful to me, soon after our youngest had died, to see all these little ones marching up and none of our own among them."

"I'd have been none too proud to have my own flesh and blood mixed up with this batch. Children of sin dressed up as smart as the rest." She glanced at Winnie Lizzie, who was now sitting in Glorermay's charge.

Ezekiel said gravely: "They children are all innocent, and equal in Heaven's sight, and meant to be loved. That's my belief, and my consolation for – for the fact that there's sin on this earth."

Without waiting for his wife to retort, he moved away towards the reading-desk.

HALF AN HOUR had passed in singing and prayers.

"The children shall now bring their offerings," Reynolds announced.

Through the chapel went a rustle of last-minute admonitions.

"Mind your sash, Cecily."

"Set they last week's lilies down gentle, Tom, or they'll scat their petals abroad."

Every pew yielded up its quota of starched dresses, clean suits, and bedecked baskets. One by one, the children filed up to the three low steps, on the upper of which stood Reynolds, handed him their gifts, then, some in a bashful scuttle, others slowly, with a smug air of duty well performed, returned to their places.

Here came the Allen tribe, Tommy hanging back. Winnie Lizzie, gently propelled by Glorermay's knee, was just behind him.

The little girl's oval face was solemn. She clutched tightly her own basket, but her eyes were fixed on Tommy's.

"Dear of en," her grandparents exclaimed in one whisper, as they leaned forward to watch her.

Mrs Reynolds leaned forward too, on her out-thrust crutch, while from the pew across the aisle Billy Richards turned to look at Glorermay.

Winnie Lizzie was mounting the first step, a yard away from our pew, when Tommy's cherries swung back under her very nose. Red, juicy, tantalising, those cherries. Her face brightened, one hand reached out –

There was a thud, a topsy-turvey vision of white knickers and scattered red dahlias and breaking eggs, and then – howl upon howl.

Ezekiel picked up the child. Blood was streaming from her cut lip, and her white dress was smeared with yolk of egg. From the smashed basket, the remainder of the eggs and honey oozed slowly over the step.

"Oh my dear life, however did ee trip?" cried Mrs Treloweth, breaking through the procession.

Between sobs, Winnie Lizzie blubbered: "Mrs Wenolds stuck her stick out – "

"Ess, she did," confirmed Billy Richards.

"Stuff and nonsense," snapped Mrs Reynolds. "Me, clumsy enough to cause an accident – in Chapel too!"

"Oh, I saw it wasn't no accident, Mrs Reynolds," acknowledged Billy. "You looked at Winnie Lizzie, then you looked at your crutch, and you stuck your crutch out right under her feet."

Ezekiel asked in a low tone: "Did you, Martha?"

"Very well then, I did," and she turned on Mrs Treloweth. "For your sake, Mrs Treloweth. When the brat was going to steal they cherries, right at the foot of the Table. Did you want me to let the whole congregation see how bad blood will out?"

"*My* Winnie's blood," began the other, furiously.

"Mrs Treloweth, you're holding up the procession."

"I'm sorry, Mrs Reynolds." Her voice was meek again, but she was quivering with rage. "I've no wish to spoil today for others as it's been spoiled for me. – Comes't on home, Winnie Lizzie, and I'll clean ee up."

She carried the child from the building.

Billy Richards kicked the smashed basket out of sight behind a vase.

WHEN Mrs Treloweth and I sat in chapel again, side by side, after the evening service, she confided to me: "I shouldn't have had the heart to come if I hadn't promised to buy they cherries for Winnie Lizzie. Had her scolding tonight, she did, and a proper one too, in spite of her poor little swollen lip. Tomorrow she shall eat her cherries, and that'll end our Festival, and good riddance to en too."

"Don't distress yourself so much about an accident that might happen to any child."

"Ah but, Miss Barton, Winnie Lizzie was left to us in trust like, and when she fails, we're failing our Winnie. Hurt me terrible, it has, that she should shame us in front of Mr Reynolds and everyone. After the pains I've taken with en, – teaching en the Gospels, and even biting off her baby finger-nails instead of cutting en, which the old folks say will stop any baby from growing up a thief. And how I'd look forward to bidding for her basket. Look, Miss Barton, not one there is as pretty."

The auction was in full swing. On the platform, Billy Berriman was proferring basket after basket; and each one, as soon as it was sold, was handed round and emptied. Most of the congregation were munching apples, peeling oranges, or cracking nuts.

"A last basket bargain," the auctioneer was now declaiming. "Grapes in en and two fine oranges, worth tuppence each at Miss Williams's – I guarantee that, for I sold em to Mrs Vellanoweth myself. One shilling. Elevenpence. Aw come on now, – Miss Williams don't want to buy em back herself, for they're that ripe they'll go poor in the night."

Glorermay, sitting just in front of us, whispered to Billy Richards: "Look, Mrs Silas has bought en; and she's sharing round. Fetch me a grape before they're all eaten."

Her escort out of the way, she threw an apple at the auctioneer who, on receiving the signal full in his chest, winked back and then picked up the Reynolds's marrow.

"One vegetable marrow that heavy that a smaller man than I couldn't lift it," he shouted. "Dirt cheap at two and six."

Glorermay jumped up, grimacing frantically.

"Aw – aw – I should have said one and six."

Up went Glorermay's hand. She slipped out of the pew as Billy Richards re-entered at its other end.

Two minutes later, she plumped the marrow down on his knees.

"Why Glorermay, whatever has took you to go and buy Mrs Reynolds' old marrow?"

"Her marrow! Tis yours and mine, Billy. Tilled it for us special, ever since June, I have. And the trouble I've had propping it up with faggots so it should get air and yet not show its underneath; and then hugging it to my chest all today – "

"But why?"

"That's why," crowed Glorermay as she rolled the vegetable underside up.

On its thick green skin were carved the initials B and G, with a heart uniting them.

"Drew it with a knitting needle I did, when this was a little fellow no longer than my hand. And the heart grew and grew with the rest of en."

"Gosh! You throwed away one and six on that!"

"Don't ee like it, Billy?"

"Oh, the drawing is pretty enough. But why didn't ee buy vegetables what are vegetables: – brocoli or cabbage or carrots or even peas – ?"

"You can't draw things on none of they."

"Glorermay! – To think I chose ee because ee seemed so sensible – " His jaw dropped.

"One do get so tired of being sensible, Billy. And though you've given me some lovely times, taking me to chapel and helping me pick blackberries and hunt for stolen nests, we – well, us hasn't done nothing very loverlike since we've been going together."

"Much good it would be, your getting used to games ee'll have no time for when you're churning, and scrubbing and baking on *our* farm."

"Reckon, by the time we get that there farm, I'll be too old for lovemaking."

"Huh! Ee will be if ee chucks your savings away on follies like this."

"Its inside isn't a folly, anyway," protested Glorermay. "Make ee a real good pie with en, your Ma can."

"Ma wouldn't waste her time cooking no such bag of water – "

"Do for pig, will it?"

"Umm. Might. Or might give him colic."

"Oh, all right. I'll put en where it belongs," cried Glorermay, snatching up the marrow.

She paid no heed to Billy's shout as she hurried up the aisle. The side door banged behind her. When she reappeared, she was empty-handed and red-eyed. Ignoring her cavalier, she came to sit beside Mrs Treloweth, and her first words betrayed where she had been.

"Do you want Winnie Lizzie's basket back, to wash and mend up? Someone's chucked it out to rubbish-heap."

"Leave en be," said Mrs Treloweth. "Old Nick can have en since the Lord's refused en."

She rose, and in silence Glorermay and I followed her out. It was growing cold. The chapel's brief holiday mood had passed. Stripped of posies and fruit, flanked only by untidy rows of emptied jam-pots, the walls looked starker than ever; draggled and dying blossoms lay trodden underfoot with nut-shells and the tinsel paper that had decked the baskets. The pagan gods had, you felt, despaired and gone, with a sigh for the harvest revels of their youth.

Not a word did my neighbours speak as we walked down the street. Suddenly Glorermay gave a little squeal. Somebody had stepped out of the shadow of a cottage and nudged her. It was Billy Richards, and he held the vegetable marrow under one arm.

Recognising him, the girl tossed her head and walked on.

"Glorermay, I say, wait. Glorermay, I reckoned you meant kindly. And I remembered that marrow jam tastes tolerable with plenty of ginger to it. So if I buy some sugar – "

In an instant, Glorermay was radiant. "Billy, what a lovely idea! I'll make it and we'll eat it together."

"Couldn't waste my money on sugar for that. I meant, we'd sell it."

Again, Glorermay's face fell, but she agreed bravely: "That would be more sensible. See if its ripe enough for jam yet. Mind how you hold en," she added, as Billy prepared to rip off a section of the symbolic heart with his penknife, "'Tis all over eggs and honey, for I dropped it right beside Winnie Lizzie's basket."

"Didn't see no basket, though I was looking with a lantern."

Mrs Treloweth exclaimed: "Why, someone must have took en in those few minutes since Glorermay came back. Anyone around, was there?"

"Only Mr Reynolds, who'd stayed behind to say goodbye to Minister and was starting up his car," replied Billy Richards.

"I'd have dearly loved to fancy as Winnie Lizzie's basket had been done honour to after all. But no, must have just got covered up with the other muck. John Peter was right: there be no blessing on showing one's pride."

"Nor one's poetic feelings," sighed Glorermay.

"You needn't be down, Glorermay, ee'll have something to show for *your* Flower Service."

"Jam, selling sixpence a pound."

Glorermay's was the tone of one who has just lost her last illusions about Love.

8

THE SWALING

"MISS BAR-TON," called Postman Crebo on my doorstep. An unusual procedure; Postman Crebo, to spare his rheumaticky legs, usually bellowed from the lane, and went on bellowing until I come out to get my mail.

He handed me a letter addressed to Mrs Treloweth. "Was you going up to they, this morning?" he shouted.

"No."

He nodded, and smiled through his beard. "As you're going upalong directly, I'll trouble you to take this here letter with ee."

"But I was *not* going," I bawled in his right ear, which was supposed to be the better of the two.

"Eh, eh? Grand weather for October. Slipped to bottom of my bag, this did, and I overlooked en. But there, when people want me to treat their business urgent, they should send it on postcards I can read and remember about."

Letter in hand, I went to my neighbours', where I found Mrs Treloweth in the kitchen, cooking and keeping an eye on Winnie Lizzie.

"You'll wait and have a bit of plum fuggin hot from baking, my dear?" she invited. "Excuse the stir I'm in. All behindhand with John Peter's dinner, I am, along of Winnie Lizzie, who's getting that strong on her legs, she's out to road before I can turn round from slab. – Now, my handsome, I'll knock your head off directly if ee don't leave eating they raw tateys. Here's something to comfort ee."

She stopped the child's mouth with a large piece of pasty, then took up her letter. "Looks like tis from our Winnie."

As she fumbled with the envelope flap, her hands trembled so that the flour showered off them. She gazed blankly at the sheets within, then passed them to me. "Would ee mind reading out what she says, my dear? Tisn't that I'm not scholar enough but – but – well, with the heat from the slab in my eyes I can't make out the sense of en."

I read out: "Plymouth, Monday. Dear Mother and Dad, You will be surprised to hear I have lost my situation, my lady being taken bad sudden, and has Doctor's Orders to go to Switzerland. Work is hard to get here now, particularly as I don't look too good, having been pretty poorly this summer. I have thought a lot lately, dear Mother and Dad. And if you will let Bygones be Bygones, I will come home for a bit and pay my board till I can see my way plainer. Expect to see me by the 7 o'clock bus tomorrow week, unless I hear from you Otherwise.

"Hoping you are well as it leaves me at present, your ever loving daughter, Winnie."

"Don't – don't mean she's coming home, does she? Winnie coming *home*."

"Yes, coming home."

"My dear life and soul!"

Mrs Treloweth fell silent, and her eyes began to water. Then she jerked her head, and swallowed. "Writes a lovely hand, don't my Winnie, Miss Barton? Top of her writing class she was, to school."

"But, look!" I exclaimed, examining the postmark, "This letter is a week old."

"Been and lost en for a week, have ey? No wonder Daniel Crebo durstn't face me with en himself."

"This means that your daughter arrives this evening."

"Tonight! And me in this stir, and John Peter's pasty not out of oven yet, and Winnie Lizzie's hair not been put in curlers. John Peter's step, that is. – Comes't on in, old dear. Our Winnie is coming tonight, John Peter!"

And as John Peter entered, she hurled herself upon him and shook him by the shoulders.

"Why, ee's all h-hot and bothered, Mary Liz," he remarked mildly, putting out earth-stained hands to hold her back. "Ee was saying as Winnie Lizzie – "

"Ee great daft gucko, you. Tisn't Winnie Lizzie. Tis *our* Winnie. Scrape they boots proper, now. Can't have her coming from a lady's house to find this place mucky."

"*Our* Winnie – "

"Ess. Coming home. By seven o'clock bus."

John Peter dropped onto a chair, and remained dumb.

While husband and wife stared at each other across the kitchen table, Winnie Lizzie helped herself to an uncooked apple tart.

Then Mrs Treloweth said suddenly: "Reckon us should put her picture to dresser to welcome en. What sez you, John Peter?"

"Ess – W-what for did ee ever l-lay en by for, Mary Liza?"

"Come last spring-cleaning, I noticed the sun was spoiling en. And seemed then as if this was the only bit of our Winnie us would have to look on again. So I thought best to treasure en careful."

She took from the dresser drawer, and opened, a brown paper packet which contained two photographs; the one of a fair, laughing child about Winnie Lizzie's age and very like her, the other of a serious-looking girl in her late teens, dressed all in white, and sitting stiffly on a chair, with trellis-work and mountains for a background.

She was propping up this one between two china dogs when John Peter touched her on the shoulder.

"Mary Liza. M-may be her'd rather us p-p-put out tother."

"Mazed, are ee? Tother hasn't got a silver frame. And this one was took special to Belruth, and the frame cost three shillings, bought new."

"T-t-tis the dress er was to wear to the Rally. Don't need to put en in mind of that, d-does us?" stuttered John Peter, going scarlet.

His words wiped the joy from his wife's face.

"I'd forgot that." She let the photograph slip onto the dresser shelf. "Reckon ee's right this-once, old dear. There'll be enough tongues and stares making it hard for Winnie to forget what is past."

She turned to me. "I'm not fancying, Miss Barton, as you haven't been told our Winnie's story. But lopsided, so to speak. And we'd like you to know it from us, would not us, John Peter?"

He nodded.

Mrs Treloweth gulped, and seated herself opposite me as if to watch for my slightest change of expression; then she began: "Our Winnie was a good girl. Brought up to be. Always top for Good Conduct marks to school, she was, after the one time her father spoke to en sorrowful like for being only second. Proud of her, wasn't us, John Peter?"

"Main proud."

"Too proud, some said, cause we kept her home till she was near seventeen, and then wouldn't put her to work nowhere but to Boskew House. But she was that pretty, you understand, Miss Barton, and us knew she'd be respected to Boskew, Mr Reynolds being a leader in public affairs and such a good man."

"Terrible l-lot the Reynoldses prized her too."

"So much so that Mrs Reynolds even left her dust they blue vases what look like them that comes from China. And Winnie never gave us cause to worry. Never hid her comings or goings, nor stayed out late, not even when Harry Jago started courting her. We was some pleased as she chose young Jago, him being then such a steady chap, and so regular to Chapel. Great lover of Chapel, our Winnie, wasn't en, John Peter?"

"Mr Reynolds and Minister himself c-called en a s-shining example."

"And Harry always fetched en back from the Girls' Sunday School Class. Things was looking all right between em. Though the summer after she started to Boskew, Winnie didn't take on like I expected when Harry stopped seeing her regular, him having got three months' work on the new road beyond Carncolomb. Came to look poorly, she did, too, and was quieter-like than usual. I thought: 'Tisn't worth wasting time with they panel doctors what gives ee half water.' So, on Winnie's Saturday afternoon off, I sent en to a Belruth doctor's to be looked at and to buy some real dark bitter medicine. Harry Jago, whose job ended that day, was to meet en afterwards and bring en home. But she came home alone, and looking awful pale. Thinking there had been a lover's tiff, I said, to cheer en up: 'Look, Winnie, here's the photographs come that was took for your eighteenth birthday last month. And your white dress what you'll wear to Sunday School Rally has come out handsome.' She, looking at me queer, says: 'I'm not going to the Rally, Mother.' I asked: 'Gone daft, have ee? You'll hold up the banner along of Faith and Truth, and Faith and Truth will sing your praises, because you stand for Purity.' She cries out: 'That's why I can't go.' Then she ran and shut herself in to her room, and us left en be, thinking she's be herself again next morning. But come morning, she wasn't there. Hadn't been to Boskew neither, and it was all in vain we searched for en all Sunday. The Monday morning came her letter, saying she'd got took on as kitchenmaid to the Sisterhood in Belruth, where they lets women work for their keep till their time comes. And that if we followed en, or sent for en back, she'd – she'd cut her throat."

"Us risked it, though," broke in John Peter. "Th-that same day. After praying."

"Ess. And when I was sent in to Winnie, I didn't reproach en, by look or word, but just asked gentle-like: 'Winnie, will Harry be your baby's father?' But she wouldn't answer. 'Own up,' I said, 'Us won't be harsh towards Harry.' Then she swore by the Bible as twasn't he. But she wouldn't say who it was. That made me feel it worse, her not trusting her own mother. I said though: 'Harry loves ee. Ask him to marry ee as ee are'. She answered, sobbing: 'I have asked. He won't. Too proud, he is.' Then she set to raving and hollering so much that the Sister said, to see us again might drive en crazy. So we had to stay away, – doubting."

"D-don't believe yet," said John Peter, shaking his head, "as twas Harry."

"But, John Peter, half the neighbourhood cried shame on en when it got abroad he'd refused to marry her. And didn't en condemn himself, taking such a turn for the bad, and knocking down poor Mr Reynolds just for reproaching en with his wrong conduct?"

"Can't credit as a darter of ours w-would swear false on the Book."

"That's a man's way of judging. Any woman knows as a love-sick girl will do, to shield her man, things no Christian would do."

"True, our W-winnie never took notice of any other chap. Tis all t-terrible puzzling."

"And terrible embarrassing too. You understand, Miss Barton, how us can't be neighbourly towards Harry, suspecting; and yet can't turn our backs on en, with nothing proved. For nothing came to light during the months of waiting. Twas the Reynoldses helped us to bear that time, paying for Winnie so she should be tended proper. And when Winnie Lizzie had been born, I was sent for, to the Sisterhood. And I told Winnie there: 'I'll even give up the parlour to your baby, against you bring en home.' But she says, 'I'm not coming home, I'm going right away to Plymouth, to live down what I've done.' Then I told en that, her being so young, we could bring en home by compulsion. But she cried out so pitiful: 'Mother! Don't make me face it among the neighbours', that her Dad and I let en have her way. She gived Winnie Lizzie to me, though, after I'd promised never to seek out the father. Us have kept that promise faithful, haven't us, John Peter?"

"Ess. Cept for s-searching the child's face."

"But there's no likeness but her mother's to be found there. See for yourself, Miss Barton."

Catching hold of Winnie Lizzie, Mrs Treloweth held close to her face the photograph of the laughing child.

"T-tis better so," said John Peter, stroking his granddaughter's hair.

"Ess. It'll help us to make believe as bygones can really be bygones, like our Winnie asks. Stop fidgeting, you little pester. Curl your hair, and wash your face proper, and put on your frilly frock, I will, against ee meet your Mammy tonight."

"I'll have to sh-shave again, to meet our Winnie fitty," said John Peter, rising. "T-two days runnin!"

Mrs Treloweth sighed. "If she'd only left us know earlier, I could have had all my new teeth put in, and met en with new sets top and bottom, like Mrs Willy Hocking welcomed her son back from Australy. Every one of her teeth drawed out on purpose, Mrs Hocking had."

"D-don't seem to me as that was d-doing right," objected John Peter. "Mrs Hocking's teeth being sound, she should have kept em to rise with on Resurrection Day."

"She's got em put by in a box to be buried with her."

"An I don't hold with that neither. Tis like tricking the Lord..."

ON RETURN from the village that evening, I found the Reynoldses' car parked in the lane outside my home. Mrs Reynolds, in her most formal attire; black silk dress, top-heavy black hat, and gold locket; was seated at the back. Her husband was bending over the car's open bonnet, humming a mournful tune, and wearing that air of infinite patience which often precedes a verbal explosion.

He straightened himself, and lifted his hat to me. "How d'ye do, Miss Barton? A most unfortunate mishap to the works, just as we was setting off to do a bit of canvassing."

"You've no doubt heard that Ezekiel is standing for the County Council?"

"Obliged to it, Miss Barton. I first said, 'What am I but a quiet man, busy enough with his duties as a farmer, Parish Councillor and preacher without mixing in County matters?' But my friends insisted: 'It's the God-fearing men whose private lives set an example, that we need on the Council.' And my wife wished it, too."

"The County Council's very respectable for a man to fill in his spare time with. And it do give some influence – "

"Yes. In my heart, I do see that a public position helps a man to help his neighbours. So I gave way, Miss Barton. And I hope I can count on your vote, Miss Barton, as you can count on my doing my duty as a Councillor by roads, water scheme, and public morality – "

"There now, Ezekiel, Miss Barton will oblige us with a vote friendly-like without your spilling election talk on her. You get that engine going."

"Reckon I'd better fetch a garage man. But what about you, Martha?"

"Come indoors and wait, Mrs Reynolds."

"Thank you. You'd best canvass The Two Tinners alone,

Ezekiel, then fetch me back later for the insurance agent and Miss Williams."

I took Mrs Reynolds into my sitting-room, and in a few minutes' time a garage car towed away the other. Next, Harry Jago knocked at the front door.

"Might I trim your garden up a bit, Miss?" he asked.

"But it is past six, and you've done a day's work already."

"Don't matter. I don't feel like quitting early tonight. Shall I pull up your scarler runners?"

"I'd really prefer you to finish the rockery."

"But they runners are that withered they're crying out to be pulled up, Miss Barton. Come and I'll show ee."

He led me to the bean patch on the western side of the cottage, and there pulled up the nearest of the plants.

Looking at the gap he had made, I commented: "Now that is done, how clearly one can see the Treloweths' cottage and the road above."

"Ess. Can't see nothing from the rockery." He added hastily: "Not that *I'm* interested in comings and goings from the bus."

His too-marked tone of indifference gave him away. Well, it was no business of mine if he wanted, unobserved, to see Winnie Treloweth arrive. I returned to my guest, only to be disturbed again, soon, by more knocks – agitated ones.

"Come in!"

Mrs Treloweth entered, breathlessly.

"Winnie Lizzie not here with ee, is she, my dear?"

"No."

"Oh my dear life, where can her have wandered to? Came down from putting my Winnie's room to rights, I did, and found en gone from the yard, and gate standing open. And her may have been gone half an hour for all I know. – Beg pardon, Mrs Reynolds, didn't notice ee was here."

"Good evening, Mrs Treloweth. I'm not surprised you are a bit bothered, what with this new difficulty – "

"Difficulty?"

"Well, it's all over the place about your daughter coming back. Awkward for you, it will be. A girl who has once slipped is hard to get back onto the straight path. You'll have to keep a close rein on Winnie."

Mrs Treloweth's colour rose. "Mrs Boskew Reynolds, I'd be ungrateful not to heed your warning after all you and Mr Reynolds have done for us. But I can't listen now, I can't. I got to go down village to search for the child."

From the window, Mrs Reynolds watched her run down the lane. "Honest, hardworking people, those, and our cleanest tenants," she commented. "But too soft. *I* say their daughter should be kept at a distance. A girl like her brings temptation to the young men. – Hum! Looks as if Ezekiel fancies he's collecting voters for the poll."

The Reynoldses' car was now snorting uphill again; in it we perceived two women's hats, one plain and black, the other poppy red.

Two minutes later, I was inviting indoors Ezekiel Reynolds, Ann Praed, and Clara Curno.

"I was on my way to return your books, Miss Barton," explained Ann. "Mr Reynolds kindly gave me a lift."

"I'm glad he obliged *you*, Miss Praed," said Mrs Reynolds, shaking hands. Then, turning to her husband, "Is Miss Curno returning books, too?"

"Um. No. Miss Curno fancied a breath of fresh air. And I promised we'd take her back down village with us."

"Fair crazy on motoring, I am, with a good driver like Mr Reynolds," gushed Clara.

Mrs Reynolds, ignoring her, whispered audibly: "Canvassing don't necessitate giving the whole village joy-rides, Ezekiel."

He warned, nudging her, "Tssh, Martha. A publican gives a powerful lead to the voting."

"That's true. – Good evening, Miss Curno. — We'd better be making haste, Ezekiel; you were a long time gone."

"As I had to wait for the car, I went along the cliff path to make sure the men had started our swaling-fires before they left work."

"Kindled all right, have they?"

Mrs Reynolds, and I too, looked through the window, out beyond my garden, westward.

The cliffs' summertime brocade of purple and rich greens had faded to russets and browns, picked out in gold where autumn furze was blooming. All day, moor and crags, windswept under a grey sky, had looked starkly sombre; but now, as far as eye could see, a faint blue haze was softening their outlines. Columns of smoke were rising in lines, at regular intervals, from the upper footpath to the north, down to near the cliff-edge. Flames pierced through and were flickering among the furze and heather.

"Wind's got up sudden, so it'll burn real fast," commented Mrs Reynolds.

"But why now?" asked Clara Curno. "I thought you didn't belong to start swaling this month, Mr Reynolds."

"We're experimenting. We want to know whether the young furze will spring up fast enough to make winter cattle food, given rain – "

"My idea, that was," interrupted his wife.

"Yes, yes. – A great help, Mrs Reynolds' interest in stock-farming is. It will leave me freer for public duties. – Why, what! Mrs Treloweth again! – "

She had rushed in. "Not been down village, her hasn't. I asked to butcher's, and Miss Williams and Two Tinners. Nor to Trewiddy lane neither. And her with her good dress not yet on and her curlers still in… Fair mazed I am, with running. And John Peter waiting upalong to go meet bus with us two, and due soon, bus is. Haven't, haven't any of ee set eyes on my Winnie Lizzie?"

"I saw her not so long ago," Ann remembered. "When you, Mr Reynolds, were giving her chocolate just by the stile to the cliff. Perhaps she followed you over it."

Mrs Treloweth broke in: "I'll run along out and look – "

Sudden perspiration studded Reynolds' face. "You can't go, Mrs Treloweth! See how the cliff is burning. – Lord, Lord, Thou knowest I went on never looking behind."

We went crowding out into the garden, towards its westward stone wall. Frightening tussles with bonfires had taught me how swiftly wind can spread flames, otherwise the sight would have astonished me. By now, the cliff was indeed well afire. The flames writhed and ran among the dead heather; from furze bush to furze bush they were flinging wreaths of gold. The wind was driving the smoke-pall ahead, and with it, red-hot thorns and twigs that fell, and set fresh ground ablaze. Sparks had settled on the tamarisks edging the cliff. I perceived that a belt of fire would soon quite cut off the stone hut, a disused coast-guard look-out, that stood on a rough platform of flat rocks and rubble about two hundred yards from my garden.

"Winnie Lizzie!" shrieked Mrs Treloweth. And then: "John Peter, John Peter, John Peter!..."

For a minute the wind dropped. An acrid smell drifted back towards us; the smoke swelled up from the ground like an exhalation and hung in a thick curtain. A solitary seagull emerged from it and flapped his way, mewing, out over the sea. A small blackened creature crept painfully across black soil – a rabbit dragging a trap.

Then the wind soughed again and the smoke surged onward, cloaking the coast-guard hut. Nearer us the iron-grey sky was reflecting the glow of the molten moor.

"Surely the little maid can't run far along the cliff?" said Ezekiel.

"Her's been to the hut and back afore. – Winnie Lizz-ie. – Winnie Lizz-ie!"

John Peter had come running down through the fields. Harry Jago now stood beside me. And a half score of women and children, evidently attracted by our shouts, had crowded into the garden.

John Peter bent forward, his hand cupping his ear. "H-hearken, Mary Liza. Tis-tis a voice from the hut."

We listened, pushing closer to the wall.

"It is a voice!" said Ann Praed.

The next cry was heard by all.

"Tis her voice, tis our Winnie Lizzie!" And Mrs Treloweth beat the stone wall with her hands.

"Thank the Lord, she can't burn in a stone hut!" exclaimed Reynolds.

His wife retorted grimly: "She can be suffocated by the smoke."

"It would be risking death to fetch her." As Reynolds said this, the blood ebbed from his cheeks, leaving them flabby and pale.

"*I-I'll* go f-fetch en!" With the words, John Peter was half-way over the wall but his wife gripped him by the collar and dragged him back.

"L-leave me go, l-leave me go, Mary Liza."

"I won't lose ee for a love-child."

"She's our Winnie's – "

"If ee go, I'll go with ee into the burning."

Ann suddenly dropped her books to the ground, and said: "*I'll* go."

Harry Jago pulled her back by the arm. "No woman could get through."

Turning to his wife, Ezekiel Reynolds said in an undertone: "It was Satan put it into your head to have them fires lit today."

She replied coldly: "It was you led the child into danger. Are you going to save en?"

Reynolds fell on his knees. "Lord, Lord," he groaned, covering his face with his hands, "Have mercy on sinners and save this innocent child."

Laying down her crutches Mrs Reynolds knelt besides him. But the glance she threw him was one of utter contempt.

John Peter was struggling to control his wife, who was tearing at her hair and clothes. Ann was murmuring prayers. Behind me, other onlookers were whispering among themselves.

The child's cries came again, louder, shriller.

Without a word, Harry vaulted the wall and headed for the hut. Those who had been on their knees rose, and we watched. Sparks fastened on his clothes, half-burnt clumps of dry plants flared anew under his tread. Then the smoke hid him. Again we were hearing only the wind and the crackle of fire.

Clara Curno broke the silence, loudly and maliciously: "Reckon that proves once and for all who is the brat's father – he what tried to shame me and kill me."

A hysterical voice cried out: "You shall hear the truth, the truth!" A young woman, a stranger, pushed forward from the group at the back and confronted Reynolds. "The truth!" she repeated.

Almost on one swing of her crutches, Mrs Reynolds placed

herself between her husband and the speaker. Then she hissed: "If you don't shut your slandering mouth – and for ever! – I'll get you put away to the County Asylum."

The last words were in a fierce understone, for Mrs Treloweth was hurrying towards her daughter.

"Winnie, my own Winnie!"

She seized the slender body in an exhuberant hug, and gazed into the face. Then she said with anxiety: "Looking some slight ee are, dearie."

"It's, it's… Oh, Mum, my head… I'm coming over faint…"

"Miss Barton'll let ee rest a bit, to her place, lovey. And directly we know if – *when*, I mean, your baby's safe back, I'll be up along with ee."

The girl allowed me and Ann Praed to lead her into Chy Byghan. I was grateful for Ann's presence, as no sooner were we inside than Winnie, in a burst of renewed and distraught strength, made for the door again.

"I must tell them the truth!" she cried wildly.

Ann laid a hand on her arm. "Now then, don't take on so. Your body will be saved. The Lord wouldn't punish ee, nor Harry, that-much!"

But Winnie broke away and ran to the open window, her thin face working convulsively. "Come in, Mum, Dad, the lot of you", she screamed, "and hear the truth."

But no one outside noticed. Instead, they were shouting: "Bravo! He's get en." – "Well done, Harry!"

We saw the young man running back across the moor, with Winnie Lizzie clutched to his chest. His face was blackened, his clothes were torn and scorched. Behind him, flames were now playing around the very walls of the hut. I ran out of the cottage in time to see him reach John Peter, who was literally dancing for joy on top of my garden wall, and place the child in his arms. A ragged cheer went up from the crowd.

When I went into the cottage again, I found all the Treloweths gathered there. The rescued child was on her grandmother's knee.

"Scared were ee, my handsome? Granny and Grandad will clean ee up proper, to home, and your Mum will come too."

But Winnie still looked agitated, so I suggested that she should rest a while longer, here with Ann Praed, her school-friend. The older Treloweths agreed, and went away, taking Winnie Lizzie with them. Now, I thought, for a breathing-space!

What a hope! Almost instantly there were angry voices and sounds of a scuffle outside.

"Stand back, Harry Jago!"

"Keep me out, would ee, hypocrites? Ee won't, ee shan't!"

The door flew open. The Reynoldses entered without a 'By your leave,' and went straight up to Winnie. Ezekiel shook her shoulder, voiciferating. "Has the devil possessed your mind now, along of your soul and body, you Scarlet Woman? – Martha, don't pay no attention to her crazy talk. Go and wait in the car."

But his wife, impassive, settled herself in an armchair, and laid down her crutch beside it.

Winnie freed herself from the farmer's grasp. Her eyes met, and dropped before, his staring ones; she stood looking confusedly about her.

Then her roving glance lit on young Jago, at the door. "Harry!"

He did not answer, but he looked hard at her.

She spun round on Reynolds. "You can't frighten me no longer, Ezekiel Reynolds. You who left your own child to burn!"

"She's mad!" He raised his right arm aloft. "As I'm a God-fearing man, may the Lord – "

"Ezekiel, stop! Taking His name in vain can't help you now."

At his wife's words, he stopped dead, with his hands in mid-air. His jaw sagged, the veins on his forehead stood out; suddenly he looked an old man. Then he mumbled: "It's true. I... I did fall from grace. Her sinful wiles overcame me. – You, you wanton, Winnie Treloweth, go down on your knees and ask my Missis's pardon."

"Chuck that bluff," retorted Winnie. "Three years back, you could terrify me. You could take me by surprise and ruin me, and then make me believe myself such a monster that, just by working in your house, I led you, a good man, into sin. Yes, and scare me into swearing solemn never to tell of that sin. Ignorant I was, then. But I done a lot of clear thinking sitting alone in the kitchen to

Plymouth, evenings, and it's showed up your bluff – "

"I... I acted according to the fear of Providence!"

"Fear of my tongue and the neighbours', you mean. That's why you threatened, if I didn't swear, to turn Mum and Dad out and lose em their work and their home – "

"Winnie – Winnie Treloweth," protested Ann, "Do you know what you're saying? You're speaking of a man who preaches The Word."

Winnie retorted: "If you don't believe me, look at his face."

Ann looked. And what that face betrayed made her cry out: "Oh Mr Reynolds! And you were our pattern!"

Winnie's strength seemed to fail her; she slipped on to a chair and sat huddled up, weeping softly.

"You're women," blustered Reynolds. "A man can only be judged fair by men."

Harry Jago stepped forward. "Will all ee've done bear judging by men's standards?" he demanded. "What about letting an honest young chap bear the blame? What about when I, being less blinded by your pious ways than tother chumps, met ee in the field-path and asked ee for truth, yes or no, as man to man? Tell em all here the pretty words you flung at me that day."

Reynolds did not answer.

"Too ashamed, are ee? I'll tell em, then. 'Get out of a decent man's way, you begetter of bastards', that's what they words was. For wasn't the Minister coming through the next field? And didn't you know as your rebukes would get abroad and shift your fault on me? Twas that day learned me that the God of all the preachings is a lie, – else he'd have blasted ee dead for they slandering words."

"Every man has a right to shield his reputation."

And a fine, charitable-looking shield you found! Refusing to summons me for assault, for fear I'd let slip my suspicions before the judges. Frightening poor Mother into letting me be packed off to Canada, to hush the matter up. Oh, if only I'd known for certain, then – "

"I – I did all for the best," stammered Reynolds, who was now swaying from side to side. "I thought on the sorrow my disgrace would cause my wife."

"A pity you didn't think of that when you first noticed Winnie's pretty face," said Mrs Reynolds.

He put his hands to his head. "I own that, Martha. But – I'm flesh and blood, and you was too sick to be a wife to me. And I've tried to even up my lapse. Never crossed you in anything since then, have I? I've been kindly and thoughtful, and let you have your fancy cattle. Haven't I kept on making ee presents of my stocks and shares, till now I've got nothing but baccy money I can spend without asking you?"

"Not too high a price for stopping my questions, eh?"

"It wasn't only that, Martha. Twas like asking your pardon and yet leaving you happy in ignorance."

"Ignorance! Bah! Some blind I'd have been if I hadn't noticed your hungry eyes on Winnie, some stupid if I'd taken your wish to support her child for nothing but neighbourly charity."

No sooner had the woman spoken than she flushed and fell to biting her lips. And when her husband went and stood over her, she cringed before him.

"You knew... all along, Martha?"

She made no reply.

"So all I gived and gived, whenever I feared you might be guessing, you just swallowed like so many bribes. And me like a mouse with a cat."

Ann uttered a little cry.

Harry Jago laughed. "Ee've spoilt your game now, Martha Reynolds. Sorry ee was too vain to hold your tongue longer, eh?"

Mrs Reynolds faced us defiantly. "A time comes when what's bottled up bursts forth, wise or not. And of course what I've said won't go no further than this room."

"Won't it? A blackmailing wife, – pretty mate for a seducer. Polverras will have some meaty gossip when you and I go forth from this room, eh, Winnie Treloweth?"

Winnie looked up. "Harry – what are you saying?"

"That I'm going to shout out the truth. The truth that I wish to God you'd told me three years back."

"Harry, please, please don't say anything."

He stared at her. "Ee was for shouting out the truth yourself just now."

"I was crazed. I didn't ought to have. Think of the talk."

"I do. You and I've suffered enough from talk. Tis the turn of the guilty."

"But – but the talk's died down a lot. And think of Mother and Dad, what have looked up to the Reynoldses and taken their wages and their presents."

"Us can't help that. The truth must be told."

"It will ruin us," said Mrs Reynolds, hoarsely. "It will wipe out all the years we've lived respected, and deserved it."

"It will be a terrible stain on the Chapel records," sighed Ann Praed.

"And me almost County Councillor, and the silver presentation cup for my thirty years' service to Temperance being given next…" Reynolds' sentence tailed off into a groan. He collapsed onto a chair, holding both hands to his heart.

"Undo his collar, Ann. Open the window, quick, Miss Barton," exclaimed Mrs Reynolds, jumping up. "It's his heart. Breathe quiet, Ezekiel. – You see that, Harry Jago. To speak will likely be to murder him."

"Harry, Harry, promise you won't speak," wailed Winnie.

His face contorted, he looked down at her, paused, and decided. "All right. After tonight, this bloody village will never see me again." And he turned towards the door.

"But, Harry, where are you going?"

"To tramp the roads."

"Harry!" She stretched out her hands to him. "Stay."

"Not without the truth is known."

"Look here, all of you," I appealed. "Don't act until you have reasoned more calmly. Is – isn't there anyone here whose judgment you will respect?"

There was a silence during which Reynolds, whose spasm was passing, looked apprehensively around him like a prisoner before a tribunal.

Then, Mrs Reynolds said: "Ann Praed is disinterested about all this."

"A worthy sister in the Faith she is," Reynolds added.

Winnie whispered: "You've always been kind to me, Annie."

"Harry Jago," I asked, "will you agree to abide by what Miss Praed says?"

He nodded. "Reckon she'll judge fair."

All eyes turned to Ann.

"I'm not worthy to advise sinners," she demurred.

"You've more grace than most here have," said Reynolds.

"Very well." She stood with bowed head for a minute, then, pale and looking straight before her, she began: "I haven't had much time to ask guidance, but I trust the Lord to send me the right words. And I speak humbly, as one who is learning that the hardest path is best. – It looks to me, Harry, you can easily prove you've been wronged. That will be revenge, which will taste pretty sweet to you, won't it? But the Lord told us 'Vengeance is mine.' And if *you* feel yourself worthy to throw stones, remember it's only thanks to His grace."

"Gosh," broke in Harry, flushing, "I'd forgot. – There's more truth in they words than ee thinks, Ann Praed."

And I alone knew that he was recalling that evening by the Watcher Crag.

"But if I keeps silent, I leaves the district," he added stubbornly.

"And confirm all the false things said, by running away the minute Winnie comes back?"

"But Miss Praed, but – isn't there no hardest path for the guilty?"

"I'm now coming to that. You, Mr Reynolds, what I've learned about you has been more of a shock than I can say. Not so much your falling, but your still setting up afterwards as a righteous man. Most would say, and I should have said myself a while back, as you should make public atonement."

"Oh, Lord! to be hounded from our congregation after thirty years' good service! For a fleeting time o backsliding – And already for three years I've been paying bitter for it. – As a preacher, knowing I hadn't lived up to my teaching, as a father what daren't fondle his own child, except on the sly."

"I can believe that, for I've been learning myself that the worst

punishment may be one that others don't see," replied Ann gently.
"That silver presentation cup will burn your hands next week,
won't it, Brother Reynolds?"

"I – I won't take it. I'll resign."

"You will take it. For I seem to be shown that that is your
hardest way. You'll be called soon enough to a Judgement
beyond – may the Lord leave you time to start atoning by your
daily life."

"Well, to leave things as they are, now that's sense," approved
Mrs Reynolds, who was regaining her composure. "Wouldn't be
just to me for him to fling away his good name."

Ann rounded on her and at last her voice was angry. "You dare
talk of justice! You, Martha Reynolds, who should be bowed
down begging for mercy on a sin twice your husband's. The flesh
led him astray for a moment, but you've been sinning through the
heart for three years, preying on his fault, in pride and greed. But
the Lord will destroy your pride when you least expect it. You just
see if He doesn't!"

The farmer's wife glared. "The Lord and I can keep our
account straight without your preaching and prophesying, Ann
Praed."

"I hope so. But as for leaving things as they are, though we may
not point to the guilty, it's our duty to point out the innocent.
And I take on myself to say for all of us here: we keep the secret on
one condition – that you and Mr Reynolds tell everybody that
you've learned for a fact that Harry is innocent. In public and in
private, you must treat him like the wronged man he is."

"I promise," said Reynolds.

His wife rose. "As for me, I've all along thought it bad policy to
heap the mud all at one door. – Come home, Ezekiel. We're
wasting our time here."

As Reynolds followed her out, he stopped beside Harry and
said in a low voice: "I... I ask your pardon, Jago. And any time
you care to drop in for a pipe or a cup of tea at Boskew, I'll... I'll
make you welcome." He held out his hand.

Harry's response was to put both his own hands in his pockets
and look away.

Winnie Treloweth who, worn out by the emotional scene, was sitting slumped in the window-seat, now took out a handkerchief and began to wipe away her tear-stains. Harry made no move to go, so I slipped off upstairs, leaving the two alone.

When a buzz of voices brought me down again, Harry was in the passage; Winnie was on the doorstep, with her parents and the child.

"And now, my handsome, supper's waiting," said Mrs Treloweth. "And as Winnie Lizzie's so near dropping asleep, I brought her down for you to see with her eyes still open. – Let your Mammy kiss ee, my handsome. – Why, aren't ee going to kiss en, Winnie?"

"Don't, if ee feels strange about it, Winnie," said John Peter anxiously. "Only, us has got t-terrible fond of the child."

Winnie listlessly took the little girl's face between her hands and kissed it. "You must teach me later how to be a proper Mammy, Mother. I'm too tired to learn tonight."

"Comes't on home, then. Dad'll tell ee what I've baked."

"M-mackerel pasties. Us remembered them's your favourites!"

"Mother, is mine a big pasty?" asked Winnie softly.

"Big as would get in oven, my old dear."

"Then, if it's all right with you, Mother and Dad, I'd like to share it." Over her shoulder she called: "Harry! You'll come and have a bite, won't you?"

He came forward, sheepish, and red-faced. "I don't mind if I do."

Mrs Treloweth's puzzled gaze roamed from her daughter's face to the youth's before she replied: "If our Winnie wants it, I reckon us can make a place for en, don't ee, John Peter?"

"Ess. – And—welcome."

Homeward they went together, along the footpath skirting the moor. Embers of the swaling were glowing like pixie-lamps, but ever fainter beneath the rising moon.

9

WHEAL GLORY

"MY ten-pound note is gone!" announced Miss Sara Lawry.

Miss Williams folded her arms on the shop counter and I prepared to wait at least ten minutes for my pound of sugar. For the wizened old spinster, who always reminded me of a crab, so hard and agile was she, was admitted to have the most active tongue in the village; and Miss Williams was undoubtedly our best listener.

"Gone! My ten-pound savings!"

"You don't say! First time you've mentioned having anything put by, Miss Lawry."

"Did I want to get the name of being rich, and be expected to give a shilling towards every tea-treat? But it's me who will be driven to accepting charitable shillings now – and all because of my trying to do my duty by my poor dying father."

"Who was buried pretty quick, I take it, seeing you're back from Plymouth within the week."

"Buried indeed! I left him guzzling steak and fried taters. I told that young woman what's married him: 'Tisn't decent; at ninety-three, a man's thoughts should be guided higher than his stomach!' But she wouldn't even once leave me alone with him to help him make his Will, so the trip's gained me nothing and lost me my ten pounds. It's clear I'm not one as is meant to have pleasures, not even pink geraniums."

"Dear, dear," sympathised Miss Williams bewilderedly. "But yours is the best parlour-windowful of geraniums in the parish."

"Yes. I couldn't bear to leave them die of thirst while I was to Plymouth. And I thought: whom could I better trust to water them than Joe Pender, him living next-door and being the only own cousin I'm still speaking to? Joe's too close-handed to go lending even someone else's property, I thought; and while Harry

Jago is away working on those new waterworks, there's no one to borrow my house-key from Joe's pocket while he sleeps. Trusted Joe like myself, I did. So I didn't risk taking my ten-pound note among they Plymouth pickpockets; I only moved it from the clock-case – which is near my geraniums – and put it to back of the tea-caddy on the dresser. And now, tis gone from there!"

"Spoken to the Constable have you?"

"Haven't, and shan't. His wife wouldn't let him oblige me by catching a thief, she's been that nasty since I asked her quite civilly if she ever washed her face, besides putting that red stuff on it. Anyhow, what can I tell? There was nothing disturbed on the dresser. I made sure no one was looking in at the windows when I shifted my note. But though I heard footsteps overhead, I did forget the peep-hole in the floor of Cousin Joe's back bedroom –the part that spreads out above my kitchen. Discovered that hole, I did, when my poor tom cat, Ginger, who was trapped last July – a beautiful mouser he was! – got shut into Uncle Joe's place. I heard him mewing pitiful, and looked up, and there was his poor bright little eye looking down near a rafter, where a knot was gone from the wood. That hole has now been blocked up, but how can I say since *when*?"

"Besides, you couldn't possibly say anything that sounded like suspecting Uncle Joe!" exclaimed Miss Williams guilelessly.

"You're right, my dear; naming names may have unpleasant consequences if it so happen that one's wrong. That's why I'm giving the thief a chance to make amends in private. Pass me a pen, will you?"

Miss Lawry scribbled some words on the back of a paper bag and handed this back to the shopkeeper, who read out slowly:

"Personal Column, *Weekly Advertiser*. 'If the person who extracted £10 from the kitchen dresser at Ivy Cottage, Polverras, returns same anonymously to Miss Sara Lawry within one week, no legal steps will be taken. Signed: Sara Lawry.' – Tis cleverly worded, but it don't seem very neighbourly seeing as everyone knows twas Uncle Joe who watered your geraniums. Why not ask him plain if he found that note, put it somewhere safer and forgot to mention it?"

"And have him accusing me of accusing him? No, Miss Williams, I never was the one to start making mischief."

Miss Williams philosophised when, her customer gone, she weighed out my sugar: "Dear, dear, I do think sometimes as to some folk plain speaking is like plain cooking, – not enough flavour to it."

DURING the next week, every Polverras conversation, begin as it might, drifted to the topic of Miss Lawry's bank-note. The unpopular little woman became, for once, sought-after: a pathetic distinction invested her. Was she not the victim of a crime so rare in these parts that even precautions against it were regarded as insulting to the community? Your wheelbarrow might be borrowed without permission, or your brocoli mysteriously grow fewer, but money was safe in your home. Front doors were never locked by night; if they sometimes were on Belruth market days 'against the gypsies', the owner's acquaintances were first told under which stone or flowerpot they would find the key. Therefore Miss Lawry's loss was a public shame.

As the week passed without bringing back her ten pounds, her insinuations became more and more pointed. She never openly accused her cousin, but her narratives laid increasing stress on that hole in his back-bedroom floor, and became more freely sprinkled with the less creditable anecdotes of his youth.

Uncle Joe gave but one sign of knowing he was under a cloud. He raised the price of his fish. He knew his public. What is twopence on a conger when the vender may let slip a significant word or glance as a clue to his guilt or innocence?

When sales decreased again, the fisherman revived public interest by a shrewd blow.

'Mr Joseph Pender of Polverras,' declared the local *Weekly Advertiser*, 'has never set eyes on Miss Sara Lawry's £10. He hereby gives notice that any person who hints that he has will be Sued for Slander.'

This challenge, in larger print than the plaintiff's, sent opinion swinging round in his favour. In those days, most people felt that a false statement in print would incite the wrath of Providence almost as surely as a false oath on the Bible. Besides, Joe must be on the right side of the Law, since he dared to invoke its aid.

From a fluent and indignant victim, Sara Lawry evolved into a patient and resigned one. Nobody could now coax her cousin's name from her lips.

Her second fling in the Personal Column was greeted as a gesture designed to end a hopeless case on a lofty moral plane: 'Miss Sara Lawry leaves to the judgement of his own conscience and the Higher Powers that person who has stolen her life-savings.'

That was on a Friday. By Monday night, the mystery was merged in a far more alarming one.

On that Monday evening, I went to the Treloweths' to fetch butter.

Ann Praed was there, making enquiries. "Father, who is a-bed with a cough, is fretting for a chat with Joe Pender. But when I went to his cottage on Saturday, there was nothing on the slate where he generally writes 'away', and today the message I had left was still there."

"Us hasn't set eyes on him, neither, for several days. And yet John Peter's seen his boat lying to Cove all this week-end. Even Harry don't know where he's to."

Ann had barely left when other seekers after Joe Pender arrived: Glorermay and Billy Richards. Billy pulled a battered cloth cap from his pocket.

"Found this to Wheal Glory yesterday, when we was taking a walk after Chapel. It's got Uncle Joe's name to its innards, and as he wasn't to home the twice we've been, Glorermay said: 'Leave it here for en'."

"That's his newer cap, what he's only worn three winters," observed Mrs Treloweth. "Where was it lying to?"

"Next the blackthorn tree, right-hand side of mine tower."

"The very spot where they found Jimmy Trevose's boots," recalled Glorermay. "Five years back that was, Miss Barton, after his sweetheart had run off with a Londoner. Both his legs and one arm was broke when they pulled his body up out of the shaft, and they knew he'd done himself in, poor chap, because suicides most always takes their boots off."

"Huh," scoffed Billy. "There was boots and hat and jacket beside Rosidney shaft when Andrew Andrews disappeared. But Andrew was in America with his blind aunt's stockingful of money."

"I don't see what either a poor daft fellow nor a rascal has to do with Uncle Joe!" objected Mrs Treloweth. "Terrible upsetting this is, though. Uncle Joe to have an accident after all they years he's set rabbit-traps up around Wheal Glory; can't hardly credit that. – P'raps he's just forgot to leave word. He'll likely turn up again, sudden, same as often. – John Peter, what's bothering ee now?"

"I… I'd rather fear an ac-cident than w-what I do fear, Mary Liza."

"Think Uncle Joe has bolted with that lippy mean old toad's ten pounds, do ee? Then I say: Good luck to en!"

"If ee'd meant to run, ee'd have run sooner," opined Billy.

"Well, he ain't so daft as to go suiciding himself down any old pit."

John Peter said haltingly, as if the words were dragged forth against his will: "There's m-men as go daft w-with conscience."

"You might!" snapped his wife. "Not Uncle Joe."

"C-conscience is a main q-queer thing what sometimes s-starts working sudden. F-for instance, at a few w-words like Sara Lawry used a-about the Higher Powers."

John Peter's troubled allusion, though the most far-fetched of the ideas that had been expressed, seemed the first to make all present realise that tragedy might indeed be looming. We avoided each other's eyes. I felt we were seeking in vain some heartening retort. Glorermay began to giggle nervously.

Billy Richards shook her into silence. In his most phlegmatic tone, he said: "Accident or conscience, I reckon that tomorrow us men should drag Wheal Glory."

A LANDMARK for miles around, Wheal Glory's derelict tower stands high on the downs, a couple of hundred yards seaward of the turnpike road, and perhaps five hundred from Joe Pender's and Miss Lawry's twin cottages. A high, square stone tower with four arched apertures, it once held the machinery by which tin-miners were lowered in cages to the diggings that honeycomb the slope. But the cages have long since been carted off for scrap-iron, and the wire fence erected to keep off children and cattle has rusted away. Today, one can easily scale the wall below the arches, and from there look down past brambles and huge ferns, down into a void that darkens from grey to black. A dropped stone, after what seems a long time, strikes water.

When it grows familiar, the tower at first glance so desolate and harsh-looking, reveals beauties. Wind and rain have mellowed its stones to hues of ochre and grey, and where the mortar has crumbled, golden and silver lichens and mauve-blossomed toadflax have crept in. Westward, the stone arches frame a narrow panel of water: blue-gold, sparkling in the sun, or grey and convulsive, spitting foam towards the clouds, expressing the very essence of the sea's varied moods.

Below the tower, blackthorn thickets slope to a valley that meanders to Trevurrow Cove. A valley where stand huge mine-waste dumps, glittering with crystals, rock-amethyst and metal-bearing ores; where rushes whisper across a lazing stream, and where, in spring, furze lies in luxuriant coils, like serpents of gold. Where, also, a few wild violets may be gathered even before Christmas.

On the Wednesday morning, I went to Wheal Glory to hunt for the makings of a posy. This was a compromise with my principles. I detest morbid curiosity and the evening before, I had cut short Glorermay's account of the day's fruitless dragging of the shaft. But thoughts of poor Joe Pender's fate were haunting me, nightmare-like mental pictures kept rising before my eyes. Telling myself I would hurry past the tower, I set out.

Clearly, the search was continuing. Some cars were drawn up by the wayside, among them, a closed ambulance from Belruth; and round the tower itself clustered a small crowd of men and women.

Glancing back towards Joe Pender's cottage, I saw Ann Praed approaching, and waited for her.

"I've just been up to Uncle Joe's in case he'd be back there," she told me. "Silly, wasn't that? But Father's got Uncle Joe properly on his mind, and that worries me; I'm so dreadully afraid of his slipping out and being told. – However, I left him dozing and he always sleeps for an hour or so before his lunch."

Miss Lawry, hovering on the edge of the crowd, detected and bore down on us. Her expression and voice were lugubrious, but the glint in her eyes hinted at a ghoulish enjoyment.

"The men are resting now, afore they have another go with the grappling-irons," she reported. "Some say there's ledges, where the shaft wall is broken, that might keep a corpse down under for good – and after me waiting about all yesterday, too!"

"How can you bear to watch?" I wondered.

"It is indeed an ordeal for anyone who suffers with nerves like mine. But I feel I owe it to Joe, him and me having played together as innocent children. I've forgiven him. Even bought new black for him, I have; skirt and alpaca blouse and a hat, what are coming out by this morning's Belruth bus. I couldn't really afford them after my loss, but I said to myself: 'It's your duty'. Poor Joe! If he'd followed my teachings on duty, he'd never have stolen from his own cousin and been brought by remorse to the bottom of Wheal Glory."

Ann rounded on her. "If you honestly believed Uncle Joe was a thief, you should have accused him to his face. Now, maybe, you're slandering the dead."

"Tut-tut-tut, Ann! I won't stay here to be insulted; duty to the dead, or no duty, I'm going in for lunch. And don't look for my face in a pew the next time you're preaching."

She made off, her gait more than ever like that of an agitated crab.

A few yards from the tower stood the policeman, and leaning against it were John Peter, Billy Richards, Ezekiel Reynolds, and several other men. Near them were heaped up rusty tins, clumps of rotten roots, an obscene-looking greenish mass that had once been an overcoat; squalid little secrets that were all the pit had yet yielded to its dredgers – and a faint stench which mingled with the scent of trodden thyme.

"He'll likely rise in ten days' time," Billy was saying. "Our dead pig did."

Ezekiel Reynolds was doubtful. "I wouldn't wager that we'll

ever see our poor brother again. Six hundred feet deep, old Miner Jenkins told me that shaft is."

"T-tis a beastly business," said John Peter. "Don't ee think us c-could let en rest in peace, Mr Reynolds?"

Challenging, Harry Jago's face framed itself within the stone arch.

"Leave en to rot like a dead dog would ee, all you pious ones? I ain't religious, but I won't do that. – Throw over more chain, Billy. I'll try the irons with another length."

John Peter stepped forward. "Ee'll fall in yourself, boy, if ee tackle it all alone."

Slowly, rather shamefacedly, the other men followed him back to their task. Further lengths were added to the chain previously fastened to an improvised pulley. A splash, a gurgle, and once more the grappling-irons slid into deep water.

The work went on in silence until a man called out: "Seems like something caught this time."

The team bent their backs for the pull. The women onlookers turned away their heads.

Harry's voice reached us muffled by the stone walls. "Heave hard, boys – the irons are loaded."

But whose were these shrill cries coming from the opposite direction?

What! – This figure bounding over the hummocks with skirts hitched up and hat askew, was Sara Lawry, running for all she was worth and brandishing a handful of torn paper.

Reaching us, she gasped: "Twas the *mousies*."

She choked for breath, then gabbled on: "That cheeky they mousies have been, since poor Ginger died. When I opened my door, I saw one running in back of my piano what hasn't been used for twenty years. And inside my piano I found his nest, and along of little pink mousies and my old butchers' bills, my ten-pound note all in shreds. See, here's bits of it. They'll give me a new one to Bank, won't they, when I've got it sorted out?"

She looked from one to the other of us, as if awaiting congratulations.

Ann told her in a shaking voice: "They're – they're dragging up

Joe Pender, Miss Lawry. If he'd been less sound in his head, I'd say your suspicions had sent him crazed and driven him to a sinful death. At the least, they shamed his last days before his accident."

The old woman began to snivel. "My poor Cousin Joe! – That he should think hardly of me at the last, and all along of they plaguey mousies. And I his best friend, and respected him even to buying new black…"

"Hi! you back there!"

"Pull harder!" rang out men's voices.

"…Joe, what was like my own brother…"

"Heave to the right…"

Ann Praed covered her face with her hands. I completely turned my back on that horrible shaft, but, too sickened to run, I remained facing the turnpike road, watching, without noticing, the arrival of the Belruth bus.

Ah! passengers were alighting, parcels being lifted out. I tried to shut my ears to the shouts behind me – until I suddenly realised they were shouts of laughter.

"Tis a donkey!"

"Silas Wills' old jackass what died of lockjaw and was pitched down shaft to get rid of en clean and decent-like."

"Drop en back quick, ee's fair stinking. – Mind they upper ledges!"

The operation had barely been completed when – Joe Pender sauntered up.

While we gazed at him in amazement, he enquired: "Whatever is all this buddy of ee doing here? – Bus has dropped a parcel for ee, Cousin Sara."

This time, there was nothing indirect about Sara Lawry's attack. Dropping the fragments of her bank note, and making clawing movements with her hands, she fairly flew at her cousin. "You cheating, lying, deceiving rascal, you. – You good-for-nothing what has fooled me twice. How dare you show your rascally skin, and me just spent two pounds on black for your burying…"

UNCLE JOE told us all that he had been away helping an old shipmate who was in sudden difficulties. What difficulties? Well–

Joe Pender wasn't the man to go prating of another's private woes. And if we fancied he'd topple down Wheal Glory by mistake, let alone throw so much as his old bootlaces down it on account of the spitefullest tongue in the world, then humankind were bigger fools than even he'd believed. Some sorry he was that Policeman Higgins had been troubled: if there was one man in Polverras that wouldn't trouble him willing, that man was Joe Pender.

His explanations were less fluent and convincing than usual; he seemed to be searching for an excuse to escape from his interrogators.

"Come upalong to my place, Miss Barton," he invited me. "I've got some real fine crabs for you to choose from."

"Afterwards, come to Father, Uncle Joe," begged Ann. "Some overjoyed he'll be to see you when he wakes up."

"Wakes – Ann, I reckon your Dad was shamming dead on ee. Tom Allen was waiting for bus, and afore I got out, I heard him tell Jim Stevens that he's seen your dad to Two Tinners, acting fair mazed. – "

"Oh dear! I must go after him at once."

She started running, making for the main road.

The fisherman looked round to see that we were alone, wiped his brow and burst out: "Miss Barton my dear, I dare speak to ee plain, and twill help my guts, what are fair heaving with vexation. What with they cats in skirts and they loonies in trousers, I ain't allowed a pennorth of the peace I needs so bad after the last four days. Saturday, I comes along quiet to Wheal Glory, looking out for a business message from a chum from Brittany, – one who don't only catch crabs. And then his boat's lights flashes a message that urgent that I runs off, not even stopping to pick up my dropped cap, and hails a lorry going to Belruth. There, to harbour, I meets my friend the Captain, and we hurries off and boards his trawler. But there's not settling the business, no, not even by dropping our burden overboard. For an upcountry Government boat comes nosing around and obliging us to waste three days off the Scillies, catching crabs what us don't want, so as to show en what ordinary, simple crabbers we be. And now, I finds the police hunting for me – in Wheal Glory! Ho, ho, ho! Carry your crab back for ee, I will, Miss, and drop a tear on my grave."

So we were soon strolling back again towards the once more deserted tower. How solid, how serene it looked now. A jackdaw was perched on its topmost broken edge, the westward arch framed a cobalt- and-silver sea. One could hardly believe that half an hour ago it had seemed a symbol of tragedy.

"Funny; thought I heard my name shouted," remarked Joe.

We halted.

"Ess, for sure. Down in the valley. Ain't they fools done looking for me yet?"

The shouts were growing more distinct. There was a stir in the bushes just below the tower, and from among them burst out a man's figure. He was advancing in a series of quick hops. – Yes, a cripple. It was William Praed.

As he hopped, he yelled: "Joe, old chum, blarst ee. Joe, I'm coming to pull ee out."

Joe Pender started running.

With the agility of an athlete – or a lunatic – the cripple pulled himself up to the wall beneath the arch. He stood there, dark against the sea: he staggered and spread out his arms...

When I looked again, Joe Pender had just reached Wheal Glory's tower. Once more, its archway framed only the sea.

MRS TRELOWETH observed that evening: "Sara Lawry's new black won't be wasted after all. William Praed being her mother's brother's cousin, she can fittily wear it to his funeral instead."

My own thoughts were not exactly lamentations either, for one must in honesty admit that some deaths are indeed 'a blessed release' – for a survivor. Would Ann, I wondered, when she had got over this macabre shock, recognise that the door to fulfilment of herself had re-opened?

10

HOUSEHOLD GODS

ON THE CLIFFS, coaxed by the sea mists and sunny intervals of an unusually mild January, young furze and litchen were masking the scars of October's swaling-fires.

In the village, the gossip stirred up by Winnie Treloweth's return had been eclipsed by newer scandals. Her past was as securely buried as any local past could hope to be; that is to say, it risked exhumation only at the most wilting of Sewing Guild sittings. And though her precise manner, learned in 'service', and her avoidance of whist-drives and socials won her a name for being 'stuck up', everyone praised the girl's quiet, housewifely ways, and agreed: she was the very wife needed by that hot-head, Harry Jago.

A touching respect marked Harry's second courtship of her. The three evenings a week when, after work, he called for her at the Treloweths', he was always wearing a clean collar and carrying a gift of flowers, and he punctiliously brought her home from their walk at an hour when most courting couples were still deep in the devious lanes.

But this had been going on for three months. It was six weeks since Harry had told me that their banns could be put up the very next Sunday, since he had secured a steady job on Oates' farm. No banns had been mentioned since then; Harry had been slipping back lately into his old morose manner, and Winnie herself looked worried and disheartened.

One evening when the lovers were parting outside my garden gate, I overheard Harry say: "A chap can't keep on waiting and waiting, Winnie. – "

"I know. – But what's our little wait compared to Dad and Mum's keeping company for six years?"

"Your Dad's the pale, patient sort of Cornishman. I ain't."

He swung off down the lane, hitting out with a stick at the hedgerow plants.

A few days later, I found him and Joe Pender at supper with the Treloweths.

I chanced to remark on the fine weather, and was surprised at the angry tone of Harry's answer: "Grand weather, ess, Miss Barton. Grand for the flowers. And the pilchers." And he stabbed the soused pilchard on his plate as if he owed it a special grudge. "But," he added, "this here green Christmas has been a cheat about filling the graveyard – not one mouldering old chump has cashed in."

"Why Harry, the gravedigger himself couldn't sound more aggrieved!"

Winnie explained: "He is thinking about empty cottages. You see, our wedding must wait until we find one."

"'Must' – that's they women's word. I begin to believe, Miss Barton, that it's not a man but cloam and a kitchen slab that a bride weds, and that, with a best tea-pot to kiss good-night to, an old maid's as happy as a wife."

"It's but fair to Winnie to wait for a home," maintained her mother. "Mean a lot to a woman, a cooking slab and dishes of her own do. Why, she don't hardly feel married without a pair of chiney dogs to the mantelpiece; when she's polishing em up, she's polishing her own self-respect. And when she puts the cloam he's broke in his lunch pasty, that's learning her husband respect."

"And going flat on her belly to clean out the flue to under slab oven, is learning herself humility, eh?" suggested Joe Pender.

"Don't ee mock, Uncle Joe. Studying her slab has taught many a woman how to master her man. For Cornish slabs like Cornish men have all got different tempers and are easier led than driven. As Miss Barton can now well testify, they're not like they up-country cooking ranges, what are so much alike ee just rents em along with the house. That us here takes our slabs along with us when we move house, shows we know their value."

"Then, it's like they heathen carting graven images about with them," objected Harry.

Winnie sighed. "Don't ee see, silly, slabs and cloam and all the rest are just signs for what a woman feels inside of her is right and proper?"

"Gosh, Winnie, I expected they ordinary country notions from your mother, but not from you."

"Why not?" enquired Joe Pender. "Just an ordinary girl, ain't Winnie?"

"Is en?"

The scrutiny that Harry directed at his sweetheart was as naive as his question. Everyone promptly stared at Winnie, and she blushed scarlet.

I thought that Joe's adjective was apt. This girl around whom the strong passions of others had fought, with such bitter results for three homes, was herself but sound country clay; decent, gentle, anxious only to be let live.

Harry admitted: "Honest, Winnie, I can't judge whether you're ordinary or not. I've always seen ee just as *my* girl."

"You've known girls a lot prettier and cleverer than me, though."

"Ess, maybe."

"Then – " Winnie's tone was sharp.

"Don't ee get jealous, my girl" advised Joe Pender. "Even a rooster, that most bigamous bird, picks a favourite out of his flock, yet can't tell no more than the rest of us, exactly how she's different from tother hens! When ee've done squabbling about the laws of Nature, maybe ee and Harry'll listen to my news. – I've got a cottage for ee."

"Uncle Joe!" exclaimed the young people together.

"Mrs Smithern told me this morning as they'd be moving to St Austell so soon as Mr Oates, who's their landlord as well as mine and Sara Lawry's, would let em go. So I goes straight off to sing your praises to Oates, Harry, laying weight on your intelligence as shown by your working on his farm for thirty shillings and refusing Boskew's offer of thirty-seven. But adding that ee was that desperate that if ee and Winnie couldn't get a home soon, ee'd likely quit the district. And Oates has promised to put Sara Lawry to Smithern's, and you'll be my next-door neighbours for five shilling a week."

"But Miss Lawry's quarter's notice?" asked Winnie.

"Sing for that her can, after paying no rent for two years. She says: 'No new roof, no rent', and Oates, 'No rent, no roof,' but the law won't let en shift her till she's got some place as good to go to, and she's found fault with every one what has fallen empty. I promise ee, though, she'll find Smithern's to her liking."

"Still, wouldn't it be quicker for Harry and I – "

Joe Pender hastily cut in: "What! Cheat me, who glories in making sacrifices, out of losing dear Cousin Sara as a neighbour after twenty years of en! No, thank ee. Besides, Smithern's hasn't but two rooms. My place and Sara's has been that mixed up one into tother since they was first built, when mine was loft with donkey-stable below – as it'll be easy to divide once more. Knock a door through my spare back bedroom, into Sara's place, I will, and give ee that room as a wedding present."

Mrs Treloweth broke in significantly: "The rooms ee'll need, Winnie, depends on whether two or three of ee are moving in."

Her words brought a sharp silence. Winnie's eyes roved from her parents' faces to her lover's, then lowered as she admitted: "Somehow – Harry and I haven't ever yet talked over Winnie Lizzie."

"Your Dad and I has," said her mother quietly. "Us'll be happy to keep the little pester. But we thought perhaps twas more proper for en to grow up along of her own mother and her brothers and sisters what'll come."

Into Winnie's face flashed the shrinking expression of one who has suffered, and fears to suffer again. Twisting her engagement ring round and round, she murmured: "I've got some fond of the kiddy. But I've never behaved like a mother to her, and I feel that Harry should choose."

"Me, Winnie? Why?"

And now she was searching his face, seeking, I sensed, to learn more of the calibre of the man to whom she was giving her life. Her parents watched.

Harry turned away from the lamplight and stared at the fire. After a minute or so, he swung round, took a big gulp of tea and set down the cup with a clatter. "Listen, all of ee. When that babby was yelling in the swaling-fire, I stood for ten minutes reminding myself as I hated en. But that couldn't stop me going in after en. And I feel a sight different about her now. She'll come along of us, and if we're ever short of pasty-meat, she'll have half mine. And now, Mrs Treloweth, I'll step outside for a smoke."

Winnie followed him, and we heard their steps going up the garden path.

"Gone to the arbor by John Peter's sty, to discuss Winnie Lizzie's eddication, no doubt," said Joe Pender, winking. "Reckon that young jack-ass has a decent man under his skin after all, though he do talk like a book-writer and a Socialist jumbled together."

John Peter nodded. "Us'll feel more c-certain of our Winnie's happiness now."

"The one thing left to arrange," summed up the fisherman, reaching for his cap, "is the shifting of Sara Lawry. Shift she will, – as sure as ever I struck a limpet from a rock."

ONE AFTERNOON some weeks later, I stopped to stare at the transformation wrought on Miss Lawry's cottage.

It had been the prettiest in the district, thanks to the big fuchsia bushes that half-filled the garden and stretched crimson-blossomed arms around the windows; thanks also to a climbing geranium on the porch and the white ivy clinging to every remaining inch of the facade.

Now, not a vestige of bush or creeper was to be seen.

The cottage wore a stark, staring coat of new concrete, marked by the mason's trowels into squares that, like tattooing on a mis-shapen woman, emphasised the wearer's lack of symmetry. A broad, straight concrete path led from the front door, and concrete had engulfed the fern-filled crannies and sparkling quartz of the garden wall.

"Mr Oates has done handsome by our Winnie. Now they mucky old plants that made it damp are gone, the place only needs red and blue glass to the porch to make it as smart as Boskew." Mrs Treloweth was addressing Joe Pender in his front garden. She was wearng her best clothes and had a resolute air.

"I'm calling to see how Miss Lawry's packing is getting along. – Come on in too, Miss Barton. That I've brought ee to see her cloam will be a good excuse."

"Hark ee, Mary Liza," said Joe. "Sit on the chair to left-hand of her slab – there's a clear space of wall there. I'll be behind en, listening in *my* indoors. And if Sara starts raising difficulties, just tap gentle-like with your umbrella."

Miss Lawry welcomed us into her living-room with a kind of sour graciousness. While the two women spoke of relatives, the weather, and the current sicknesses – a formality that precedes every correct local business discussion, for ten minutes at least – I looked about me.

That room was an epitome of what the house-proud in Polverras admired. Its slab, large enough to cook joints for ten people, was flanked by a dresser crowded with cheap china; and more china dogs, shepherdesses, souvenir plates and 'present for a good girl' mugs stood upon or hung from stools, shelves, wall-brackets, and hooks. A purple china minstrel had had to find standing-room at one end of the kitchen table.

"Worth seeing, Miss Lawry's cloam, ain't it Miss Barton?" asked Mrs Treloweth with honest admiration. "I suppose, Miss Lawry, they pink plates with the yellow pheasants and blue daisies on em are your company ones."

"Oh, I never *use* any of what you see here; my using cup and saucer and plate are out to scullery. But I've not let a day go by, these twenty years, without dusting em, no more than I've missed polishing my slab that I only light once a week. That'll tell you how I value them, and how much relieved I am to have three months clear for their careful packing-up."

"Three months!"

"Yes. I said to myself, What's the need to hurry out, now that Mr Oates has done up the place so nice? So I've been and paid up my back rent to Mrs Oates, and for all she's a little simple-minded, her receipt is good in law, and now I'm entitled to a quarter's notice."

"But Winnie – "

"I'm sorry, but I'm sure you quite see as I must consider my cloam."

Mrs Treloweth tapped softly with her umbrella on the wall.

For a few minutes, the two women discussed with growing heat the respective claims of daughters and cloam.

Then a bang on the wall startled us. Every article on the dresser quivered. A second knock almost shook one of twelve florid milk-jugs from its hook and at a third, a plate slipped sideways.

Miss Lawry jumped up and clutched the dresser with both hands. "Joe's gone crazy! Fetch him in, quick, before every bit of my cloam is scat abroad."

He duly came, carrying a very large hammer.

"Some sorry I disturbed ee, Cousin Sara. Been meaning to put up a matter of a few shelves for a long while, I have, and now that fishing's slack I'm making a start."

"How long will ee be on the job?"

"Umm, well – I'm a clumsy-handed fellow when I gets on shore. Fussy about having things straight, though. If they shelves should tilt the first time and the second time, they'll come down and go up a third time."

"But my goodness, I'll have to stick by this dresser all the while you're knocking, for I've no place else to put the cloam."

"Then ee'd best bring your bed alongside of en, Sara, for I'll be working according as I've time, may be morning, may be nights. On and off for weeks, may be. If I might suggest en, Sara, maybe your cloam would be safest in a packing-case."

And he turned on his heel. Very soon milk jugs and saucers were dancing again.

When we took our leave, Miss Lawry said, with tears of rage in her eyes: "Mrs Treloweth, perhaps as I'll be moving on Friday after all."

We congratulated ourselves on a rapid victory.

We had forgotten that in every good local housewife's heart her cloam is rivalled by her slab.

IT WAS Friday. The next day, Winnie and Harry would be quietly married in Chapel.

On my way to the turnpike road I caught sight of a mattress wobbling above the level of the hedge ahead. Rounding a bend, I came up first with John Peter, who was pushing a creaking wheelbarrow, the load on which was covered by a sack, then with a farm-cart piled with furniture and led by Billy Richards. On a chair perched on the driving-board sat Mrs Treloweth, balancing in her lap a china toilet-set.

"We be getting their home ready against they come into en, tomorrow," she greeted me. "Harry is working today, and Winnie had to go to Belruth. But all the furniture us has bought cheap to auctions being so big tis awkward that Mr Oates can only spare the cart for one trip. – That mattress a-pitching on my head, is en, Miss Barton? – I can't turn to see."

The mattress looked so threatening that I climbed onto the cart and held it in place for the rest of the journey.

"The old toad must be well gone," opined my companion as we drew up. "Silas Willy's wagon, what went up at eight o'clock sharp to fetch her things, is no longer here."

As the cottage seemed deserted, we walked in without a second glance.

A shock awaited us. The furniture was still in its place. Miss Lawry, surrounded by packing-cases labelled 'China', was sitting with her hands folded in her lap, looking at her slab.

"Silas Willy not been?" demanded Mrs Treloweth.

"Been, and been sent away," answered Miss Lawry tranquilly. "Quite forgotten, I had, that my slab is too big to get out of front or back door. It came in twenty-two years ago, through a door that is now bricked up."

"Then bust told door in, ee must."

"If that door isn't unbricked very careful, the house 'll fall down. And the masons are so busy that they can't say when they can come and do it."

For a moment, Mrs Treloweth looked nonplussed. Then she offered: "Miss Lawry, I won't say nothing about your spoiling a poor young couple's wedding just from a spirit of contrariness. Give ee a generous deal, I will. My Winnie's new slab, which is ordinary-sized, is now outside on barrow. Ee shall have en, and leave your old one here."

"Leave my slab, that I've polished every day with a silk duster, to be mucked up by a giddy young wife! My gracious! – I'd sooner go on sitting and sitting here, with my poor cloam all packed up. While my slab stays, I stay."

"Us'll go see what Uncle Joe can suggest."

When that sage had heard the story, he reflected, then asked: "Mind old Peter Griffiths what lived to Cousin Sara's place twenty-five years ago, do ee, Mary Liza?"

"Who grew so fat he couldn't get upstairs?"

"That's en. And what is now Cousin Sara's living-room was his death-room. And they couldn't nohow get his body out for burying, so they made bigger the coffin-hatch left in the floor above, for ordinary- sized tenants' corpses, and hoisted Peter up into the loft, what is now my bedroom, and out through the wide door what is still there."

He moved away to hold a consultation with John Peter and Billy Richards. These two then went into Miss Lawry's, Joe ascended his own stairs, and Mrs Treloweth and I waited in the road.

Very soon, high-pitched cries of rage brought us hurrying back into the living-room.

The slab had been torn from the wall, in which a sooty recess now gaped. It stood in the middle of the room. Above it, between the rafters, boards had been removed to leave a hole three feet wide and the length of a man, and over the edge of this, Joe was beaming down at us. He dangled ropes, the ends of which John Peter and Billy Richards were fastening round the stove, taking no notice whatever of Miss Lawry's gibberings and her frantic tugs at their sleeves.

"Hurry and hoist en, boys," directed Joe. "Poor Cousin Sara's fair fretting to be gone."

They heaved. The stove began to rise.

"You'll hurt en, ee'll utterly smash en, as ee tried to do my cloam," wailed its mistress.

Spitting soot from its crannies, the ungainly iron stove reached the level of our eyes. A last heave, a last lurch and shower of smuts, and it vanished into the room above.

Miss Lawry stood under the coffin-hatch gazing alternately

upward and at the void in the wall. Her face was twitching, but she was evidently now past speech.

"Billy and John Peter'll pull our furniture off the cart," called down Joe Pender to her. "Then us'll load your slab straight on to en through my epps door, and Billy'll drive en to Smithern's. And some glad I am that I could help ee out of your little difficulty. – Make haste, Cousin Sara, if ee wants to drive with the slab."

Miss Lawry snatched a hat and coat from their pegs, and scurried outside.

Not long after, we heard the cart drive away.

Then Joe Pender rejoined us, smiling beatifically. "Reckon that's squared up my little account with Cousin Sara over that there ten-pound note," he chortled.

"Twas a cruel rough way to treat a fine old slab," commented Mrs Treloweth.

"Ah, Mary Liza, ee don't know the best of it yet. That slab *won't go into Smithern's neither.* Not by the front door. Nor by the back, until there's cleared away a heap of old tins and rubble and muck that's been piling up outside some fifteen years. That sure of diddling us and not moving at all, Sara was, that she didn't take much stock of Smithern's. Reckon her slab'll spend next week in the garden – and tis coming up for rain."

"Poor soul!" ejaculated Mrs Treloweth.

I am not sure whether her compassion was for the woman or the stove.

11

THE PLAGUE

THE JAGOS' nanny-goat was sick. Harry, hearing that I had once spent a few weeks on a goat-farm, had called me in that evening to give an opinion on the case, but I had failed to suggest even a new diagnosis.

Glorermay and Billy Richards too were shaking their heads over the patient.

The little black-and-tan goat was a pathetic sight as she lay there stretched out on straw in a lean-to shed. Sacking was tied over her flanks, now so thin and heaving so painfully; her long eyes were watching with indifference our efforts to help her.

"After all, Harry, might have been cheaper to call in vet to en," said Billy Richards. "There's shillings-and-shillings-worth of different drenches been wasted down that goat's throat by now. If I was you, I'd slit her throat."

"But I sure wouldn't dare face Winnie afterwards. Such a pet she and the child have made of the poor beast. Why, she'd hardly quit fussing around with blankets and hot drinks, to go Belruth this afternoon. Ee knows what a woman – "

"I know what a woman will be if she isn't handled firm," retorted Billy loftily. "Well, I'll be getting along, and so should you be, Glorermay. It's spotting with rain already."

"Oh dear, so it be!" exclaimed Glorermay. "And me left the Missis's wheel-chair out to road! She'll be mad if the new leather seat gets spotted just as I'm bringing en back from the repair-shop. Can ee give me something to cover en with, Harry?"

Harry provided straw from a pile in the shed-corner, and the cripple's chair was brought in and padded. Glorermay had just pushed it to the yard gate when she looked up the road and paused.

A car with a lorry in its wake was approaching.

"Gracious, me not back yet, and here's the Missis already back from station with His Serene Highness. – Eh, Uncle Joe, come quick and look at him."

Joe Pender sauntered out from his own porch, newspaper under arm.

"His Serene Highness by Champion King out of Reine d'Or," chanted Glorermay in an awed tone. "They say his blood is purer than the Prince of Wales' own, and he comes direct from Guernsey where the King himself talks French when he goes visiting."

The vehicles were halting opposite us. We could all look our fill at the young pedigree bull, latest of those costly additions to the Boskew herd that for weeks past had been the talk of the district.

No doubt of it, he was a distinguished-looking beast. His muscular dun body filled two-thirds of the big lorry, barely leaving room for Jim Andrewertha, Boskew's chief cowman, to stand at his head. But you forgot his bulk in admiring his build; the clean line from forehead to rump, the neatness of the small dewlap, the arch of the deep ribs.

His Serene Highness was obviously used to being stared at. He stared back with a bored expression, then shivered and snorted, as a few drops of rain fell on his back.

"How do you like my Missis's choice of beef, Miss Barton?" asked Reynolds, leaning across his wife so as to forestall her greeting. "Cost us a pretty price per pound, it has."

"When he brings us in guineas per pound weight in a year, what with stud fees and the extra value of the calves, you'll be praising my marketing, won't you, Ezekiel?"

The farmer sat back and did not speak again. He now, I noticed when meeting them together, made few attempts to parry his wife's nagging. He showed signs of ageing, too, and was growing unhealthily fat. Martha Reynolds, on the other hand, had lately seemed younger and more vigorous with every week. Today, she looked proud and elated.

As more rain fell, she called out: "Put the blanket on him, Andrewertha. – Lucky I came with you men, or you'd be letting four hundred and eighty guineas' worth of prize stock catch his death of pneumonia. Don't ee know yet as pedigree bulls is as delicate as young turkeys? – And you, Glorermay, I expected you to be back, seeing to it that the men had his stall fixed proper. Get in the car. Andrewertha shall rope my chair in the back of the lorry. – Careful now, Andrewertha, mind it don't fidget the bull."

"My! she's letting me off lightly," whispered Glorermay, before she climbed in. "I hope His Highness keeps en in that lovely mood."

But the expression that had just crossed Mrs Reynolds' face was not of good humour; it was tense, as that of a gambler who has flung his last shilling on the cloth.

While they drove slowly away, Harry, looking after them, mused: "I've read, Miss Barton, as bulls were put in churches in the old days, and men bowed down to em. Maybe the notion wasn't such a crazy one. Look at that woman and that man and then at the beast."

"The beast's a fine beast," agreed Joe dryly.

He opened his newspaper again and was reading it while we all went back to the shed. Of a sudden, he gave a whistle.

"Any stirring news, Uncle?"

"Herring prices is up. A foreign chap's knifed a girl in Plymouth. Oh um – and the foot and mouth disease has broke out again among the cattle in Somerset. Some to-do they Government meddlers are making about en. Fines or prison if ee conceal a case. Ruining farmers they are, for every cow or goat or pig on an infected farm must be slaughtered, and the Government only pays for em at market prices."

"Needn't worry us. The foot and mouth hardly ever crosses the Tamar."

"Still, it's carried terrible easy, by bedding as well as by beasts. Described here, the symptoms are – Harry, I don't like the way that there goat keeps on dribbling."

"A proper nuisance it is. She's messed up near all the packing-case straw that Miss Williams gave Winnie. We'll be short of bedding for en now that Glorermay's taken what we'd used once and dried again."

"U-mm. Come from up-country, they packing-cases, don't they?"

"Taunton, I believe. Miss Williams generally sends em back, straw and all, but Winnie – "

Again the older man whistled.

"Listen, boy – if anything should happen to that goat unbenownst to ee, Winnie couldn't blame ee. And it would be a good thing."

"Why? Do ee think – ?"

"I don't think, leastways, not aloud. It's too risky a habit, here where what's done by mere accident be often put down to spite. You remember that, boy! Now, will ee oblige me by running down to Two Tinners with they mackerel for the Curnos. I want to pitch a sackful of rubbish down Wheal Glory afore dark."

NEXT DAY, Glorermay told me that Winnie had come home to find an empty shed. The goat had died soon after our last visit, and had been quickly disposed of in an unmarked grave, so that her mistress should not sorrow over her remains.

FEBRUARY had turned cynical and was deriding the hope of spring when, one afternoon a fortnight later, I started off for Boskew Farm with a message for Glorermay. The puddles reflected an ash-grey sky. The sparse early celandines were cowering. An east wind blew across the moor and with its whistle blended the chafing of a sea that looked as if it would never be blue and calm again. It was not, however, to wind, clouds, or sulking sea that the day owed its grimness, the countryside its air of desolation, but to the silence and emptiness of the fields.

At that hour, cows should be lowing their readiness for the milking- shed; Treglown's grey donkey and her foal nosing hopefully around the cottage garbage-heap; the Hoskens' pigs disputing the mangel-wurzels now rotting undisturbed in a corner of the Hoskens' field. The golden-fawn of the Boskew Guernseys' coats should be lending colour to sodden meadows.

But today, for miles around, not a single cloven-hooved animal was out under the open sky. Plague was on the land. The new bull at Boskew, shortly after his arrival, had developed foot and mouth disease, infecting others of the herd. On the farm and all neighbouring ones, all stock was stabled and under Government rule.

At the top of Boskew Lane, a Belruth policeman, stationed beside a large enamel basin filled with whitish liquid, was arguing with Joe Pender and the Treloweths.

"Regulations is, M'am, that no one comes in or out of the infected area without stepping into this disinfectant."

"I shouldn't be frightened but it'll give us all our death of colds," said Mrs Treloweth, gingerly putting out her foot. "How many more murders do your old Inspector want on his mind?"

"Murders, M'am?"

"Regulations it may be, but I call it fair murder to slaughter all they poor cows, sick or sound."

In Joe Pender's opinion: "Government'll soon be telling us to put Winnie Lizzie in a coffin so soon as Tom Allen's Gertie gets the measles. And that'll be 'Infant Welfare'. Whenever they M.P.s leaves the jobs we pay em for – getting top prices for Cornish brocoli and chasing Dutch trawlers out of Cornish waters – they makes a mess and calls it by a fancy name."

John Peter nodded.

"With all their schooling, they can't even find out how the foot and mouth infection got to Boskew," said Mrs Treloweth.

"No. And won't. That mystery will stay as deep as Wheal Glory," declared Joe Pender.

We were nearing Boskew House, and, at short intervals, sounds like gun-reports were falling on our ears.

"Hark!" exclaimed Mrs Treloweth, "They're still at the killing."

My companions hastened their steps, and before I realised where we were making for, we approached the meadow in which the slaughtering was taking place. It was one of those opening out of the cattle-yard. In the yard itself were loitering a dozen neighbours and farm-hands, among whom was Glorermay, seated on an upturned pail and with her face buried in her hands. Just within the gateway stood the Reynoldses and the government inspector. At their feet there yawned a wide trench that ran the entire length of the meadow and beside which were placed, at intervals, petrol-cans and piles of dry brushwood. Looking along that trench, I saw the golden-fawn of hides.

Butcher Vellanoweth was dismantling his humane killer. His work was done. He had carried out the death-sentence on a herd whose value, said rumour, amounted to many thousands of pounds.

Jim Andrewertha told John Peter: "I had the leading of em out. It would have fair torn my heart away if they'd been, rightly speaking, the Master's cattle."

He glanced covertly, from under his thick grey brows, at Martha Reynolds. Several side-looks followed his, and more than one betrayed a gloating spite. But it was a spite tinged with respect.

"She's meeting her ruin with her head up, I must say," admitted Joe Pender. "Pale as chiney clay, but not so much as a twitch of the lips to show us what she's feeling."

"She's been there for three hours. Standing, too. We was allowed to make firewood of her chair, because it had stood in the infected stable."

An involuntary movement of sympathy brought me closer to the group by the trench. The Inspector was asking Ezekiel: "Can you assure me, Sir, that there are no more cattle anywhere on the place?"

"So far as I know. But ask my wife, who has been my stock manager lately, since my health has got so bad."

The woman replied simply: "Look."

She raised a crutch and pointed to the cowsheds, where gaping doors revealed row upon row of empty stalls.

"Just as a formality, Madam," said the Inspector, "I must give a last glance round the buildings myself."

"One question before you go, then, Mr Inspector. Are you really absolutely sure that there's no extra compensation for pedigree stock?"

"I tell you once again, Mrs Reynolds, that the Government pays current market rates for slaughtered beasts. If they're worth more, well, it was up to the owner to insure them."

Mrs Reynolds moved to the very edge of the trench and stood

there, looking down, still erect and composed. Her gaze lingered on the carcase of the pedigree bull.

Then: "Fire it," she ordered Andrewertha.

As she turned away, she seemed suddenly to wilt; she missed a foothold and tottered. Her husband steadied her.

"Come indoors, Martha," he urged. "You never should have insisted on watching that most painful sight. How providential, though, that you'd just insured the herd."

She stopped and, looking him full in the face, said slowly: "It was not insured by a penny piece."

"Not insured! You told me that that three hundred pounds – "

"I meant it for insurance. But just then Serene Highness came onto the market. Too good a bargain to miss, I judged. So, as the bank wouldn't extend my overdraft, I put the premium money towards the bull's cost."

"Well, well, well! An even bigger disaster than I guessed." But there was surprisingly little distress in his tone. "Some lucky that the farm itself wasn't my freehold to make over to ee, Martha, for we've still got that."

"Yes, yes, and your brocoli and taters," she said bitterly. "Go on, Ezekiel. This time, I can't say nothing back."

"Martha, I'm not going to reproach you, my money though it was! – Perhaps we can pull together better now that *I'm* the farmer again."

He threw back his shoulders, and his supporting arm drew a little closer around his wife's waist. Master once more? – I doubted when I glanced at Martha Reynolds' tight lips.

They marched on, seemingly unconscious of everybody near them. Behind them, the petrol-soaked brushwood, now piled on the trench, took fire with a crackle. Flames roared up, but to be swiftly cloaked with thick, dark smoke tainted with the smell of burning flesh.

The Reynoldses were half-way across the yard when, around the corner of a shed, dashed a cow. A singular-looking cow. She was thin and dirty, with parts of her coat shaggy and parts clipped short; stranger still, on her flanks and back were large patches of a purplish hue. The government inspector was in full chase after her.

When he stopped for breath, she stopped too, trailing a broken tether just out of his reach.

He fairly exploded: "What's this, Mr Reynolds? 'Every cow dead' and one walks in at the back door while I'm going through the sheds!"

"That's no Boskew cow," said Mrs Reynolds emphatically.

"Looks like a stray from a circus," guffawed Reynolds.

"She's the shape of a Guernsey and she's on your ground," retorted the official. "Have her caught. Call the slaughterman back."

Jim Andrewertha made an unsuccessful lunge at the cow, who ran into the field, was brought to a momentary standstill by the evil-smelling smoke, and then lost her wits completely and dashed wildly up alongside the trench. A ten minutes' pursuit was ended by Andrewertha's return, grumbling, coughing and rubbing his smarting eyes.

"We'll catch the beast and dispose of her when she has quieted down," proposed Reynolds.

The Inspector replied: "My duty, Sir, is to see that not a beast remains alive when I leave; in fifteen minutes from now, if I'm to catch that Truro train for Launceston. And I'm sorry to say it, but I daren't leave anything to trust on this farm."

"Why not?" demanded Reynolds, flushing.

"Frankly, Sir, I'll have to write none too good a report. You delayed giving notice of the outbreak, you wanted to try goodness knows what outlandish local 'cures', and now there's this fishy stray-cow business – "

"That's enough!" said Reynolds in a fury. "*I* dodge the law, indeed; I, a preacher, a J.P. and a County Councillor! To show you, I – me what's got Doctor's orders to take things quiet, – I'll damn well catch that cow myself."

And he started running.

"Ezekiel… stop, you fool!" called out his wife.

But the warning came too late. Overcome by excitement, the unusual exertion and the smoke, the farmer almost immediately collapsed.

Andrewertha and John Peter lifted him, and carried him between them into the yard.

"Lay him in the parlour," directed Mrs Reynolds. "Ann Praed's there, sewing – she knows what to do for heart. And send for Doctor – "

"Madam, let me help you indoors." The Inspector offered his arm.

But Martha Reynolds jerked his hand from her sleeve. "No. Not yet. – Think only a man can put duty first, do ee? My girl has a knack with the cows – Glorermay? – Where's Glorermay?"

Glorermay was at that moment in a corner of a shed, to which I had pushed her in an effort to conceal her hysterics. For the last quarter-hour she had been wringing her hands and looking inexplicably agitated, and when Reynolds fell, she had given a wail and burst into tears. Now, of course, I must needs bring her forward.

"Fetch that cow," ordered her mistress.

"Suppose she runs away to cliff, M'am?" objected the girl, in a tone that was almost defiant.

"That cow, Glorermay, will be brought in afore I stir from here, even if I stay till I drop."

Glorermay's defiance melted into consternation. "Oh-h. Oh Lor! – That on my head too, what's maybe got the Master's death on en already... B-uuh!"

She ran sobbing into the meadow, whence her voice came back to us. "Bet-sy, my andsome! Bet-*sey*!"

A few minutes later, girl and cow were confronting the inspector; the cow with her head slipped under Glorermay's arm and nuzzling at her apron pocket. "Here she is, Mr Inspector. Here's Betsy whose next calf Mrs Reynolds promised to give to me and my young man, to start is farm with. Awful cruel it seemed to kill en, and her as fit as a fiddle and sleeping two stables away from the sick bull. – I thought if I disguised en what with shaving en and putting on a whole five-shilling bottle of hair-dye; goodness knows why it's turned purple when it makes Cecilia James' hair that lovely black; and tied en to cave down under to Cove, till the trouble had all blown over, why, she could come

back as a surprise like. And Mrs Reynolds'd have en to start again
with."

The Inspector sighed and wondered: "Does anyone in Cornwall
ever help the Government to carry out its work?"

"Not if us can help it, Sir," was Glorermay's ingenuous reply.
"Ee see, we feel that if our own ways aren't perfect, well,
Government's are always worse, so what's the sense of trying
Government's? And all have gone off beautiful, it would, if Betsy
hadn't got impatient waiting for me to bring her supper. – Oh
Betsy, fair done yourself in, ee has, my lovey. – Take en, Sir; but
do ee please promise as she shan't be butchered right in that there
stinking smoke, – she'd be that scared."

The Inspector promised. And he added, human nature getting
the better of official: "I'm sorry it has to be done, my girl. I – I like
to take a sporting chance myself, sometimes."

WHEN, later, I made my way home with Ann Praed, I asked her:
"Is Mr Reynolds very ill?"

"Yes! – It'll be terrible for that proud woman if she loses even
her home."

"What do you mean?"

"Boskew Farm is leased on Mr Reynolds' life; as they did use to
lease places here, Miss Barton, when country people were scared of
putting their names to papers. So when he dies, it goes back to the
landlords: and it's well known hereabouts that they have a quarrel
with Mrs Reynolds and won't renew the lease for her."

We went up Boskew Lane, while gusts of reeking smoke blew
across our path from the slaughter-field.

As we looked over a gate at the fire that now outlined the grim
trench Ann cried out suddenly and nervously: "Miss Barton, it's
sometimes terrifying to be that close to the Lord that you read His
words plain and *know* they're going to come true. I can see what
they flames are spelling out. I see: 'And the proud and sinful will I
cast down'!"

12

FINAL RECKONING AT BOSKEW

A FEW DAYS later Ezekiel Reynolds was improving, but might be abed for many weeks. Through Glorermay, Mrs Reynolds accepted my proffered loan of an air-cushion for his use.

When I took the cushion to Boskew, I met her on the door-step, dressed for going out.

We were talking when Ann Praed came out of the house. "Mr Reynolds would like to see Miss Barton," she said.

Mrs Reynolds pursed her lips. "He's already seeing more company than Doctor would approve of."

"Yet Doctor said he mustn't be denied his fancies. He got quite excited when he heard Miss Barton's voice."

"What's over-exciting him, Miss Praed, is your Bible-reading and preachy talk. Next time he sends for you, please answer you're too busy to come. It's his duty to me to lie quiet and let his heart steady."

"But isn't it my duty as a Christian to go to a sick man when he asks for me?"

"Sloppy kind of Christianity that is! If Ezekiel needs a preacher all the time dangling round his bed, he might as well have stinking powders and guttering candles, too, and own up that at heart he's one of they Papists."

Both women's nerves were frayed. To avert a theological squabble, I suggested: "Shall I see Mr Reynolds for a few minutes only?"

Ann led me indoors.

The front parlour made a depressing sick-room. The big brass-knobbed bed in which Reynolds lay stood in the piano's old place under the picture of the family grave. The blinds were lowered. Dust-sheets shrouded the carpet. The two huge blue vases flanking the hearth more than ever evoked funeral urns.

The invalid looked up from a large Bible which was open on a table beside him. His eyes were feverish and he greeted me with but a wan attempt at his old joviality.

"You said you wanted Miss Barton for some private business. So shall I leave you?" Ann asked.

"No, no. I'll need you too. As the Missis is gone out, now's a good chance. Yet I don't know as there's such a hurry, after all. Doctor's saying that my next bad turn will be my last, don't mean it's bound to come soon, do it?"

"No," answered Ann. "Besides, those who feel fit to meet the Lord needn't worry if His call is sudden."

"Quite right, quite right. – But them that ain't…"

"You, Brother Reynolds, don't need to ask such a question; you who only last Sunday spoke on 'The sinners shall perish'."

"But, Sister, you yourself have preached some pretty sermons on hell-fire texts; yes, creditable sermons for a beginner. But always allowed in your heart, haven't you, that the translators had got a bit beyond themselves about the burning?"

"Oh, no! Why, it's all or nothing with faith. 'Except a man believe, he shall in no wise be saved'!"

The girl moved closer to the sick-bed. How grave, how taut she looked standing there, the mourning she wore emphasising how much paler and thinner she had grown since the shock of her father's death. She looked full into Ezekiel's face.

He turned away his head. His lips were twitching and after a few minutes' silence, he asked: "Shocked ee just now, didn't I, Ann?"

"It was your sick brain talking, Mr Reynolds. You believe. You know you do believe."

"Ann… say a prayer for me."

She took his hands in hers. He muttered: "Do ee shut your eyes, though. They bother me, those born preacher's eyes of yours; seems like they're telling me that the burning's coming close."

She closed them then, but her clasp tightened, and she seemed to be putting forth strength as well as seeking it as she pleaded: "Lord, Lord, give this poor brother courage. Don't let him deny his faith."

There was another silence. Then a tremor shook the sick man and quickly and loudly he said: "I believe! Willing or not, I believe. *ALL* – even that the whited sepulchres shall receive the greater damnation. I won't die the Pharisee I've lived, Lord; I'll do what I meant... Ann, fetch... fetch..."

His voice trailed off and he slipped lower in the bed. "Water..." he murmured. "I'm in they hell fires now..."

As I handed Ann a filled glass, I whispered: "Remember! Excitement may give him another seizure."

The look that she turned on me startled me, mingled so strangely in it were a revivalist's zeal and the shrinking of a bewildered girl. She whispered back: "I – I'm scared myself, Miss. But if tis his soul against his body, why, I *must* help him fight for his soul."

I made no further protest. After all, a stranger could not fathom the needs and the fervours of these emotional Celts!

Reynolds was pulling himself up on the pillows again. He instructed: "Ann, fetch out a brown paper packet what's back of the sideboard where Glorermay hid en for me. And open en here on the bed."

She obeyed.

The wrappings fell away. And what they shamelessly laid bare was the warping of a sentimental heart.

What a medley of worthless trifles: a rattle labelled 'my eldest son's', a wedding favour, a school certificate in Reynolds' own name; then newspaper announcements of the births and deaths of Martha Reynolds' seven children, and that of Winnie Lizzie Treloweth's baptism with the surname inked out and 'Reynolds' written above it. And a crushed basket; why, that too was Winnie Lizzie's, the one that had vanished on Harvest Festival night.

A photograph slipped out. I saw Martha Reynolds in her wedding dress, with 'My Wife' and the wedding date written beneath; saw too, a coarse gibe pencilled from head to foot.

Reynolds flushed, and turned it face downwards. "Twas done one night when I'd wanted to take her in my arms and she would only nag, nag about the men's wages. – Eh, here's what I want."

He pulled from an envelope a closely written sheet of paper.

His hands were shaking. "Listen: I wrote this the night after the swaling-fire. But twasn't till Doctor told me how I might be called sudden, that I decided to finish en... and even so, I'd changed my mind again until Ann prayed just now. It do seem hard that my fine reputation should be busted up when I'm dead and can't even enjoy living free of it. And after I've followed that road of silence that you counselled, Ann. Its paying twice for one set of sins."

"But what is this paper, Brother Reynolds?"

"My confession. Queer, ain't it, – I what hate to be caught in my sins by men, yet feel such a powerful need to confess em to men. Do that show I'm no born humbug, only a made one? Or be it a Popish yielding to a weakness of the spirit?"

The girl answered with bowed head: "With sudden death in front of ee, you must do what the voice inside ee bids."

"Then I'll sign this, and you and Miss Barton – who's got the only other tongue I can trust – shall witness as I've done so when sane and of my own free will.

"And after?" I asked.

"Ann shall take en, and when I'm gone, she'll give it to the Circuit Superintendent, who if he thinks fit, will publish it abroad. – Perhaps," added the penitent with a perceptible gleam of hope, "if tis still Superintendent Elvers, he won't think fit; a broadminded chap, is Elvers. But I'll have done all I could to atone for my transgressions. – Read it aloud, Ann."

She read: "'The Confession of Ezekiel Daniel Reynolds, an unworthy servant of the Lord.

'I have preached the Word to gain praise, and without following its teaching.

'I, a Rechabite, have broken the pledge and taken strong liquor in Belruth and other places where I safely could.

'I have sinned by the flesh with Winnie Treloweth, an honest girl; and by pride and love of my fellow men's esteem, in not acknowledging the fruit of that sin.

'I have made impossible any practical amends to those I thus injured by giving all my worldly goods, in fear of her tongue, to that worse Pharisee than I, my wife – '"

"Stop!" I exclaimed. "Mr Reynolds, your faults are your own to confess, but–"

"Too hard on Martha, am I?" he retorted sullenly. "She'd have been a good wife to a man what would flog her silly, or to one that hadn't no pride in him at all. But ain't it she who has badgered me into living a lie? Don't I feel her hate like a hand on my throat every time she comes near to this bed–"

His voice was rising. Suddenly, checking himself, he lifted his hand. "Listen, she's back! – Go, both of ee, keep her outside. I'll deal with they papers. This once, she shan't best me. Go quick!"

EVIDENTLY Mrs Reynolds, on her return, had met Mrs Treloweth and Winnie Lizzie coming up to the house. She was saying: "I'm sorry, but Doctor's orders are: No visitors, no flowers."

"That's some pity. Winnie Lizzie was spending the day with us, and I got en to pick they anemone buds herself, for her chum, Mr Reynolds. I thought a sight of the child would brighten en up."

An odd call behind me made me turn. "Chuck, chuck, chuck, chuckie – " Reynolds was reeling in the open doorway.

The child recognised the play-call and darted to him. He lifted her in his arms, turned, and staggered back into the parlour. The three of us hurried after him.

"The papers," whispered Ann, pointing to the hearth.

There, no doubt flung in haste after the rest, Martha Reynolds' likeness was turning to grey ash.

Ezekiel now lay sprawled across the bed, and Winnie Lizzie, laughing at this new game, was clinging to his knees.

Mrs Reynolds snatched the little girl and literally flung her across the room.

Glaring into her husband's eyes, she cried: "You fool, fool, fool!".

He groaned; and then he slipped slowly to the floor and there lay very still.

After one glance at him, his wife turned and stormed at Ann. "Look! That's what your preaching and praying has done. Made me a destitute widow, you have, you nosey, stuck-up, sanctimonious chit! Look, and then get out!"

Ann bit her lip hard; then she hurried, weeping, out of the house and away up Boskew Lane.

EZEKIEL REYNOLDS had lingered on without power of speech for five days. His funeral had wrung even from Mrs Reynolds' worst enemies the tribute that she had buried him handsome, and now the sale at Boskew House was taking place.

This was the most important local auction for a long time. Almost every wage-earner in the village had sought time off to attend it; householders with feeble dependants dragged them along too, rather than stay away. When I arrived, in the pouring rain, I found Mrs Willy Jenkins soothing her four-weeks-old baby in the shelter of the porch, and Miss Lizzie Curno was extracting from her senile grandfather's pockets the shiny kitchen spoons he had collected when her back was turned. Tobacco smoke, stale-smelling steam exuded by wet coats, and the drone of many voices drifted out together through the front door; and the passage was crowded with people who were brushing from their clothes the crumbs of picnic lunches.

Never during the Reynoldses' tenancy could Boskew House have rung to so many cheerful voices, yet never had I seen it looking so forlorn. The spirit of despoilation pervaded it. Glorermay had, I knew, stayed scrubbing and polishing till midnight, so that visitors might find no flaw in her mistress's housewifery: but already the furniture was patterned with hand-prints and the floors with those of muddy boots; already Bobby Tonkins Junior and a pal of his had decorated all the wall-space they could reach, with blue crayon cats.

Gossip was dwelling on the slowness of the bidding.

Sentiment plays a big part in country sales: a popular labourer, turned out of his small holding, will get twice their value for his broken chairs and home-made tables. At this one, the proceeds of which would go to a much-hated woman, the crowd had come to finger, to chatter, to criticise, but not to buy.

The auctioneer, who had started at the top of the house, so as to warm up enthusiasm before reaching the best pieces, was now coming downstairs.

Some fifty people squeezed themselves into the parlour with him. He mounted a chair and, with an air of determined optimism, began to extol the mahogany suite. In its entirety, he declared, it would add an ancestral dignity to any home.

There were several sniggers.

"Ain't anyone told that poor emmet as there ain't another house in Polverras as would hold it all?" wondered Mrs Treloweth.

Piecemeal selling commenced. Sideboard and table fell to a Belruth dealer at a ridiculously low price.

"This auctioneer don't know how to handle the women," criticised Joe Pender. "He should feed em strong slops, to get em that stirred up in their innards as they don't know what they're doing with their purses. Old Trewinnis, now, would have given even that there fender a sentimental value, and had em all believing as the late owner and his missis sat over it cooing like a couple of sweethearts."

"It goes to my heart to see a good sale bungled," sighed Mrs Treloweth.

"Bargains is better than excitement," pronounced John Peter. "Us might even get Mr Reynolds' Bible ch-cheap. Twould be g-grand to see en sitting on top of ours."

"You don't try no Bibles till we've settled they blue vases," said his spouse firmly. – "Why, Miss Lawry, didn't notice ee alongside of us. To your new place, you ain't got an inch of spare for any more cloam, of course."

"Well – " Miss Lawry's eyes narrowed as she calculated. "I could just make room for them vases by moving a chair into the back kitchen, and they would round off my collection nicely. Of course, they're not worth much now; I remember hearing as how your Winnie cracked one of em when she was working here."

"Our Winnie never cracked nothing, that's why Mrs Reynolds trusted her to dust they vases every mortal day. And why, too, she'll be so proud and pleased if us can bring em to her as a surprise present, for memories' sake."

"Clara Curno's after them also. For her new home, as she calls the two rooms at the Two Tinners that she and Billy Berriman are setting up in."

"What, are those two children going to be married?" I exclaimed.

Miss Lawry gave that little hitch to her jacket which is her signal of a full-scale verbal attack.

"Yes. I gather as Clara was counting on an older bridegroom. I can't pass on a mother's confidence – but I do think Mrs Curno was sensible not to go bothering either that Belruth garage man nor the traveller what took Clara they moonlight picnics, since Clara herself couldn't decide which of them she had the most claim on. And Billy, who's anxious to start his nice soft job of bar-tending, is willing to fix the wedding date early enough for Clara to wear the dress she wanted. Satin. A *white* satin – "

"I don't see it's for us to criticise what colour she chooses," said Mrs Treloweth tartly. "Neither us as is happily married, nor us as has never been given an excuse to think of wedding dresses, nor even layettes – "

Miss Lawry aimed a pained look at her, and retreated.

"Er'll force they v-vases up sky-high in price now, out of t-temper," prophesied John Peter.

"Her shan't get em, no, and nor shall Clara, the little hussy. – Ain't they handsome?"

She edged her way nearer to the vases, whose merits Clara Curno was pointing out to her fiancé: "Almost like that one which Lina La Vida kept her lover's heart in, ain't they, Billy?"

"Dunno. Wasn't me who took you to that picture."

"Ee needn't look so jealous. Isn't leading me to the altar enough for you? And the fine home you're getting – I got Ma to realise that as the bridegroom isn't much to make a stir about, we must make a good show of the home, and I've fair pledged myself to bring back they vases."

"Perfect specimens after a design of ancient Pekin – " declaimed the auctioneer.

He could have saved his breath. Most of his audience had never heard of Pekin, but every woman among them, bar myself, could see beauty in those vases, or at least in the gentility they symbolised. And their very uselessness raised them above the level of common things, where husbands still have the right to urge economy.

The first bid was one pound for the pair.

"Twenty-two and six," offered Clara.

"Twenty-five shillings," said Mrs Treloweth, her eyes bright with rivalry.

Miss Lawry went sixpence better. Two or three other bids were made, and the price rose by sixpences to thirty shillings.

"Thirty-five shillings," called out Clara.

Miss Lawry capped it with another shilling.

"Her voice has gone silky; tis a sure sign she's set on getting em," sighed Mrs Treloweth. "Thirty-seven shillings."

"Liza, Liza," protested John Peter, "us has got that new shovel to buy."

"And hasn't us sacrificed more than a shovel for our girl before now? We'll eat taters all week, if need be, and stay away from Chapel if there ain't sixpence left for collection. – Thirty-eight shillings."

Miss Lawry added sixpence, Clara, a shilling.

"Two pounds," cried Mrs Treloweth, her voice breaking.

There was a pause.

"That's my last fling! Miss Barton, do ee pray with me as they'll stop now."

"Forty shillings, offered. Any bid for forty-one. Forty it is. Going, going – "

"Forty-five," said Clara serenely.

"Forty-six," spluttered Miss Lawry.

The duel continued between them in thrusts of one shilling.

With every thrust, the old woman looked angrier, the girl more sparkling. Patently, Clara meant to squeeze as much glamour as possible from a destiny more prosaic than the one of which she had dreamed. Her pose, her tone, her enjoyment of the limelight were all foreshadowing that opulent matron who, a few years hence, would be ogling customers across The Two Tinners bar-counter, while her husband and the children who bore his name discreetly stayed in the kitchen.

Finally, the vases were knocked down to her for three pounds.

When most of the attendance had followed the auctioneer into the kitchen, Miss Lawry still lingered in the parlour doorway, and

Mrs Treloweth, with tears of disappointment reddening her eyes, approached her successful rival.

"Clara – if ever ee should get tired of en, will ee give us the chance of buying it off ee cheap?"

"Right-o," Clara agreed good-temperedly. "Too antique for my taste they are, really, but I bought em because, to start off with, they'll get my home admired like nothing else would. And of course I shall modernise em, – stick our yellow sofa crooked behind em, with Oriental cushions on it, and put a few red tin dahlias in one and have one of they jazz-coloured jointed snakes popping out of the other. Wonder how I could best fix his tail into it."

She tipped up one of the vases and looked inside it.

"Hullo! What's this old junk down here?"

She plunged her arm in and drew out a bundle of crumpled papers, some basket-work.

Mrs Treloweth craned her head. "My goodness gracious! Tis Winnie Lizzie's Flower Service basket!"

So Ezekiel had not burnt all his secrets. Instead, he had thrust some into this temporary hiding-place. Here was a predicament: if I said nothing, the story would tell itself; if I said too much, I might start a train of scandals worse than the truth.

Clara was eagerly rummaging. "There's writing too," she announced, pulling out the handwritten sheet. "Look, Billy."

"Aw, Mr Reynolds's own hand. I ought to know en, after all the cheques I've cashed for him at Miss Williams'."

"But why our basket along of en?–"

I intervened. "By chance, I know these are private papers and for whose care they are intended. I can't say more – but if you will give them to me, Miss Curno, I'll put them in the right hands."

"But they're mine now. Who buys an article buys whatever happens to be inside it."

I glanced around. Miss Lawry was creeping nearer, making pretence of examining the pictures.

After all, that grotesque confession had done all the good it could, by soothing the trouble in Ezekiel's soul; what could it do now but harm? I made up my mind. "Miss Curno," I urged, "you,

I'm sure, don't need to be told that an honourable lady, if she wouldn't give up those papers, would burn them at once."

The implied compliment told on Clara, and I could see she was yielding – until Miss Lawry's voice chimed in: "Burn em! Do no such thing! – begging your pardon, Miss Barton. Why, that there may be another Will. The one person who should see it is the widow, and I'll take it to her."

"I could take it myself," rejoined Clara.

Miss Lawry sidled up and put a hand on the girl's shoulder. "Clara, my dear," in her smoothest tones, "your own business is enough for you to worry about. I'll do this little errand for you willing, just to show I don't bear any ill-feeling about the way you bid against me for they vases." She turned to Billy. "Your fiancée and I has been friends ever since her christenin, Billy Berriman. So close we've been that perhaps I know more about Clara, and why Clara's marrying you, than even you yourself do."

Billy looked surprised. Clara's start showed that the veiled threat had not missed her.

It was urgent that those papers should burn; at once, in any of these empty grates. I slipped off to the kitchen in search of a box of matches to give force to my exhortations.

If only, instead, I had sent Billy for those matches! – The kitchen was crammed with people and I had to push my way to the match-holder.

On re-entering the passage, I saw that Miss Lawry had triumphed. She was showing the paper to Miss Williams. "Like your advice I would, Miss Williams my dear. There's something here I doubt I should trouble poor Mrs Reynolds with just now, in the sorrowing state she's in – "

Within half an hour, there was not a man or woman in that crowd but knew at least one version of the story.

When the confession finally reached Martha Renoylds and she declared that Ezekiel, out of his mind when he wrote it, had followed the usual pattern of madness by turning against a beloved wife, nobody chose to believe a word she said.

NOW the Treloweths were leaving the house. John Peter was

silent, his feet dragged and his underlip trembled incessantly.

His wife whispered to me: "Oh, Miss Barton, that awful proud is John Peter! Why, ee talked of tearing up all the clothes they Reynoldses gived Winnie Lizzie, and spitting on em once each for each 'Thank ee' we've said."

IT WAS six o'clock. The sale was over, but not till next day would most of the furniture be taken away. Mrs Reynolds was sitting alone by the kitchen table.

Catching sight of me in the doorway, she called out: "Why, Miss Barton, you ain't surely coming to say good-bye to me? You'll be the only one."

But when I went in and sat down too, she remained gazing straight ahead of her.

At last she said as if speaking to herself: "Him so weak and I so strong! Yet he's bested me after all. He's taken away everything I married him for, even a respected name."

Glorermay came in. "Your taxi'll be here in ten minutes, M'am, and M'am, may I say what I've been thinking – "

"Well?"

"It don't ardly seem honest of me to take that month's wages what I ain't worked for, instead of notice. And I was wondering who's going to do for ee when e've done visiting your sister to Belruth and goes to that there little ouse to turnpike?"

"I shall have to break in another slattern, I suppose," said her mistress grimly.

"Because, if ee'll have me, I'll be some pleased to go on doing for ee again, until Billy and me marries – and Billy ain't in no hurry for that. Tisn't for the money. Mrs Polglaze what ain't so far to go to, did offer me two shillings a week more. But you've always meant well by me, M'am. And I don't like to think of ee getting someone what'll leave ee when you starts scolding her for her own good."

Mrs Reynolds reflected for a few minutes. "You may come. But you'll be a house-parlourmaid and must wear your white apron every afternoon, and learn to get it less mucked up than you do now."

She put out a hand awkwardly and, looking in the other

direction, patted Glorermay on the back. "Thank ee for offering, Glorermay".

And then the lonely woman broke down into tears.

13

POSTSCRIPT: WITH PRAYER, PASTIES
AND PHILOSOPHY

THE DEATH of my landlord had broken the lease of my cottage together with that of Boskew House. My revived good health and energy had for some time past left me no valid excuse for postponement of my return to life north of the Tamar. And so this was my last Cornish evening.

I was enjoying it in the garden, looking out at the Cornish sea; at the Cornish countryside, that land without winter, where autumn mates with spring. Primroses were peering jauntily from among shrivelled bramble- leaves; brown fields where the brocoli harvest had ended contrasted with gold-studded green ones where that of the market narcissi was in full swing.

"Good-night," I called out to a passing farmhand and reminded myself: Tomorrow I must lose this friendly habit of greeting passers-by. Tomorrow –

The gate clicked. It was Joe Pender, dangling a still lively sea-bream.

"Tis said, Miss Barton," he informed me, "that fish sits solid in a stummick even when that stummick's being pitched about in a train. I ain't experimented myself, hardly eating fish, in a manner of speaking, except for every day a couple of mackerel or herring, what ain't really what us means by *fish*. But I brought ee a bite for breakfast."

He carried it into the kitchen and, while I sought a large deep basin, accepted my invitation to sit down. The bream stowed away, he still made no move to go.

"Expecting company tonight, are ee, Miss?"

"No."

"Well, you're getting em. Hurried to be first one in, I did, seeing as real lady though you are, Miss Barton, I count ee as a friend. And neighbours and good-byes to friends don't mix too good. Not to my mind – nor to other minds either, – that's where ee'll see a bit of sport, I'm thinking".

Barely had he spoken than Ann Praed arrived at the door. Her radiant face prepared me for good news. Joe Pender deliberately forestalled her in its telling.

"Good luck to ee, Ann. Tis a proper step up for ee, being asked to speak a few words at Gwennap, come Whit Monday."

"Yes. I had thought you'd be pleased to hear it from me, direct, Miss Barton."

I congratulated her whole-heartedly, knowing the prestige of the annual open-air service at Gwennap Pit, that great amphitheatre, set among meadows where John Wesley himself had preached.

"Ee may get a hearing, if there aren't too many toads."

"Toads, Uncle Joe?"

"Fair swarm in those meadows, they do, after a soft wet winter like we've had this year. Last Gwennap service I was to, two of em was hopping among the seats, and what with the girls squealing and the boys helping em hitch up their skirts, not a word of the preaching could I hear – not till the policeman arrested they toads and put em in a paper bag."

"Toads or not, I mean to get listened to," smiled Ann. Then she lowered her voice. "Miss Barton, I – I've got a favour to ask."

Realising that she wished to speak to me alone, I led her into the garden. From there we caught sight of the Treloweths approaching across the fields.

"Oh dear! And I put off coming here till so late, just from hopes of catching you alone, Miss Barton. You see, they others wouldn't – understand. But you, Miss, you do believe, don't you, that a prayer can help, wherever it's said?"

"Certainly."

"Then I wish, even if it's said in a church with images, you'd put up one for me at Whitsun. Don't ask that I'll speak well at Gwennap – I know I shall. But, that I shan't feel too pleased with myself, for, inside, I'm fair bursting with pride and joy. About everything – even the new hat I'm buying for Gwennap. And that's quite wrong."

"It's quite natural."

"But after the bitter lesson my first chance brought, I do want really to deserve this second one." She signed towards the Treloweths, who were drawing near. "You see how stuck-up I am, not wanting to tell my failings in front of my neighbours! The tools are in my hands, I know, but oh! Miss Barton, do ee think I'll ever be fit to use them?"

I encouraged her: "Don't worry. Only remember, Miss Praed, that you are still very young."

My last glimpse of her was on her way up the long lane, with the long hill before her.

The young Jagos, who had taken a short-cut, joined the Treloweths almost at my gate, and they came in together. All were casting unusually glum looks at each other. Winnie carried a basket; Mrs Treloweth a dish wrapped in a cloth.

"John Peter and I were now coming to bid ee good-bye, Miss Barton, my dear."

"So was Winnie and I – not thinking to bump into anyone." And Harry returned his mother-in-law's accusing glance.

The occasion clearly called for a cup of tea all round. We had one. And we talked. And we had another cup each. How long would they all be staying? I began to wonder as nine o'clock drew near and none of them had yet started "good-byes".

Nor had they half an hour later, when Glorermay joined the party. In her turn, she looked none too pleased to find company; and she also carried a parcel – of half-moon shape, unmistakeably a pasty.

A faint smell of hot pastry and potatoes was drifting up from Winnie's basket and her mother's dish. All my guests had been sniffing covertly, in all the women's eyes lurked a sparkle of – could it be suspicion? Or even jealousy?

At last, Joe Pender winked at me and enquired: "All taking hot pasties for an airing, eh?"

Glorermay began: "Mine's –" then gulped and stopped. "Forgot, I did, ee made me jump so, Uncle Joe. Tis between Mrs Reynolds and Miss Barton."

"If Mrs Reynolds is sending a private message, us can go stand on doorstep while ee gives it," offered Mrs Treloweth stiffly.

Glorermay was embarrassed. "Tisn't my fault. But, 'Don't let no prying noses near it', Missis said; beg pardon all, but she did say it. And she would bake en herself, though as she let me chop the meat and onion, tis part my present too. She says it'll stay with ee well for lunch in the train, Miss Barton."

"Stay more'n that, it will," Mrs Treloweth predicted witheringly. "That solid, Mrs Reynolds' pasties are, as ee could pitch em down a mine-shaft and fetch em up again, looking no different."

Harry plumped the basket on the table. "The wife and I wanted ee to have a real tender one, Miss. Went to Belruth myself, special, I did, for good steak, as this sure is."

And another pasty emerged from its swaddling-clothes.

"Winnie! Ee didn't say nothing of en to me, your own Mum."

"No – o, Mother. Harry thought – well, us thought: Miss Barton having been so kind, we'd make her a little gift on our own, thinking it would be the only one, since you don't belong to bake pasties on a Tuesday."

"As if, after all the bouncing old times Miss Barton has had along of me, I wouldn't change pasty day, and washing day, and burying day too, if I could, to please en! Many of my pasties you've eaten, Miss Barton. But this I'd made to do ee proud, – tis no forty-and-one with forty pieces of tater to every piece of meat. Swedes, and extra onions cause we knows ee likes en. And a wallop of cream mixed in, eh, John Peter?"

"Ess. I told Mary Liza: 'Don't be sparey of nothing'."

"Look at the beauty!" and Mrs Treloweth unwrapped the biggest pasty I have ever seen.

Then, with a resentful air, she began to wrap it up again.

"Suppose us will eat en to home as ee've already got two, Miss Barton. For to do justice to en, my pasty should be eaten lunchtime tomorrow, while he's still crispy-fresh."

"Winnie and I had pictured you starting on ours at just about Plymouth," said Harry. "But of course Mrs Treloweth's –"

Glorermay asked anxiously: "What shall I tell Mrs Reynolds, Miss? Her not having many pleasant things to think on now, poor dear, she do get that snappy if her little plans don't go exactly as she meant."

I sensed that on this minute depended the memory I should leave behind me. Desperately I said: "I shall enjoy all of them, all for lunch." Then I blushed at my own idiocy, for one single pasty is for me a square meal. Not, apparently, for my listeners, though.

Harry warned, in earnest: "Different makes of pasties fights awful inside of one."

"Tell ee what, old dear, eat the one what looks best to ee, first, and write and tell us which twas." And Mrs Treloweth, cheering up, gave me a confident nudge, like an artist who is certain that his work will win the prize.

Joe Pender grinned. "Write to all of ee, Miss Barton will, I bet; and so tactful that each one fancies hers was best," he predicted with disconcerting foresight. "And a nice exhibition of the 'One and All' spirit ee've given her, staying on and staying on, each hoping as tothers would leave ee be last, so ee'd get a bit of special praise in private."

There was a chorus of denials.

"Anyhow, if us was a little hurt," admitted Mrs Treloweth, "twas because if it's only a little old pasty, still, it's like a bit of life here, what we're leaving with a friend."

"Life, eh? Ess, reckon a pasty's like life all right, but not only life at Polverras," mused the fisherman. "Tough meat for the work, and soft taties for the bed and comfort, onions for the unexpected happenings and a bit o salt where ee gets a laugh. And a good thick crust over all, to make en look better to the neighbours than it really be. Eh well! Tough or tender, don't make much difference when tis digested."

"Clara Curno wouldn't hold with that notion of life," said Glorermay. "For a jealous one, that's her; fair driving her Billy daft because she can't go to London too and run around the shops and the Chamber of Horrors. She says there's no Life here."

This puzzled Mrs Treloweth. "There's preachings and treats and whist drives and socials and funerals, ain't that life? What say ee, John Peter?"

"W-why, the Lord's put life everywhere! Even to burying-g rounds t-there's birds and worms."

Harry laughed. "If Clara's thinking one can't be happy in this village, I had that notion once, sure! But I'm cured of en. Ain't I, Winnie?"

"Clara means Life with a big L like they spell it at the Pictures," explained Glorermay. "Forgot the half of what she told me, I have. But twas something about Fate and Seven Sins and whole lashings of virtues what the hero and heroine always has. Don't get none of they here, she says."

Through my mind flashed a series of scenes from the past year.

"Tell Clara," I said, "to look under the crust. And tell her that life with a big L is just the same old pasty – but it often costs more. And too often it doesn't taste, as ours here do, of the sea and the earth. – But Clara won't understand."

Nor, I think, did several there that evening understand; far less would have many of my city-bred friends. But nor would I have wished to have it spelt out to them. They had sufficient wisdom, and in straining for more they might have lost that begotten of sea and soil.

And then their mother country would no longer have been the refuge to which I dreamt of going home one day.